Having bravely undertaken a subject usually left to preachers, psychologists, and criminologists, Richard Armour feels he must establish his status as an authority:

1. He was once (though he hates to admit it) a teen-ager himself.

2. He has a Ph.D. in English Philology, and thus understands the speech of present-day teen-agers — when they speak slowly and distinctly, which they seldom do.

3. He has, for several years, studied his two teen-agers and their incredible friends with scientific detachment and only an occasional shudder.

In spite of these demanding activities, he has found time to teach at a number of colleges — currently at Scripps College in California — and to write 27 books, including many, such as **It All Started with Columbus** and **Twisted Tales from Shakespeare,** which are favorites of teen-agers.

Susan Perl is well known for her illustrations in **Vogue, The New York Times,** and elsewhere.

D1497653

McGraw-Hill Paperbacks by Richard Armour

The Classics Reclassified

It All Started with Eve

Twisted Tales from Shakespeare

Golf is a Four-Letter Word

Through Darkest Adolescence

with tongue in cheek and pen in checkbook

Richard Armour

with illustrations by Susan Perl

McGraw-Hill Book Company

New York Toronto

ACKNOWLEDGMENTS

I should like to thank the editors and publishers for permission to include verses which first appeared in *The American Legion Magazine, Better Homes and Gardens, The Christian Science Monitor, Collier's, Family Weekly, Good Housekeeping, Look, McCall's, The Saturday Evening Post, Together, The Wall Street Journal,* and *Westways.* I am also grateful for permission to use portions of my article, "How to Talk to Teen-Agers," which appeared in *American Youth.*

Contents

Prologue:
My qualifications as an authority

Most of those who have written about teen-agers have been psychologists, criminologists, dermatologists, men of the cloth, or singers. Being none of these, I would seem out of my depth, if not out of my head, in approaching such a complex and baffling subject.

But I have several rather remarkable qualifications with which I wish to impress the reader at the outset. Having gained the respect due me, I shall then be able to proceed without having my statements questioned.

In the first place, I was once a teen-ager myself. I hate to admit this, and until now have told only a few close friends. But someone (I suspect my mother) must have talked, and I have the uncomfortable feeling that my secret is out.

"Wouldn't you like to look at some pictures?" I can imagine my mother asking people with whom, at some cost, I have built up a reputation for respectability and adulthood.

"Yes indeed," these people reply, because they cannot very well say anything else, my mother already having opened the large photograph album and thrust it under their noses.

The picture of myself at six months, stark naked on the sofa, with a piece of oilcloth under me that was more practical than aesthetic, embarrassed the devil out of me when I was in eighth grade. But the picture of me in eighth grade is the one that makes me slightly ill now. In this (unless, as I have always hoped, the negatives got mixed up and it's really a photo of someone else), I am thin, pimply, stooped, with a silly expression that bespeaks a vacant mind or no mind at all.

All right, then, I *was* a teen-ager once—but only once. When, at last, I became an adult, I remained an adult. There may have been a few backslidings, but they were brief and harmless, and I prefer not to discuss them.

At any rate, my experience as a teen-ager is something which, once I overcome my reluctance, I can draw upon. Of course, my own adolescence was so long ago that it might be thought to have no pertinence today. It has, I confess, very little, but there is a generic resemblance. Like the modern teen-ager,

I, too, was troubled by the first stirrings of sex, though not until I was about fourteen. Up to that time I thought there was no difference between boys and girls except that boys could run faster and throw a ball farther. Also, girls were always putting their hands up in class, and not just when they wanted to leave the room. Nowadays boys begin getting ideas about girls when they are ten or eleven, and by the age I was starting to catch on they are already going steady.

Then there was acne. It started with me just at the close of World War I. When others were celebrating the Armistice, I was just beginning my own seven-year war with my epidermis. About the time the Germans laid down their guns, I picked up a small device for squeezing blackheads which was seldom out of my hands until the final months of the Coolidge administration. Today, when I see an adolescent with a bad case of acne, my heart goes out to him. I want to say, consolingly, "You won't believe this, son, but I once looked just as repulsive as you. In four or five years you'll be over it." However, I restrain myself, prompted not only by my natural reticence but by the likelihood of his making some such hostile remark as "Whacha starin' at, Bud?"

I had only a light case. A light case of acne is like a light case of the plague. It doesn't kill you, but it worries you plenty, and it gives you a slight idea of what those go through who have the real thing.

I remember a period of several months when I didn't want anyone to see me, and I stayed in my room as much as possible or went to the movies, where it was too dark for even the person sitting next to me to notice my spots and bumps. At the movies, too, I forgot my troubles, becoming intensely interested in the passionate love scenes of the hero and heroine, neither of whom had acne.

I tried everything, including mud packs. Nothing did much good, though the time I answered the doorbell, forgetting I had my mud on, took me several months to live down. My Aunt Emma, who had a remedy for everything, said the trouble was my diet.

"The worst things for your complexion," she said, "are nuts and chocolate." It was almost as if she knew that my favorite food was, and still is, chocolate-covered nuts. Her telling me they were harmful made me like them all the more, and what had been a pleasant desire became a passionate craving, to which I yielded several times a day.

It was this same Aunt Emma who advocated scrubbing with soap and water. "Cleanliness is next to godliness," she used to say, though for several years I misinterpreted this expression, and with good reason. You see, the time there was the most insistence that I scrub my neck and clean my fingernails was on Sunday, before going to church.

Gradually I came to take the condition of my skin for granted, helped a good deal by the fact that most of my companions looked as bad as I did and several looked worse. As the years passed, so did my acne, and the time at last came when I could look back on the whole business as nothing more than a nightmare.

Another thing about my experience as a teen-ager. Before I reached adolescence I went through a period when I was sure my parents were not my parents. I was certain I had been adopted, after having been left on their doorstep or acquired by this kindly couple from an orphanage the way a mongrel is rescued from the pound. By the time I was convinced that these strangers were really my parents, a time which coincided roughly with arriving at my teens, I had a rather low opinion of them, and it was with a feeling of dismay, followed by stunned resignation, that I accepted the blood relationship. Such was my sense of shame at about age thirteen, that I would probably have concurred in some lines I wrote many years later:

Sons and daughters in their teens
Think their parents don't know beans.
This is bad enough, although,
Even worse, it's often so.

All this—the discovery of sex, the battling with acne, the downgrading of parents—is, I am told, normal. In a way I am sorry, because I hate to think that what I endured during adolescence is the experience of millions of young persons who, in each instance, think their misfortune peculiar to themselves. On the other hand I am also glad, for purposes of this book. My subject, which at first I had merely thought nauseating, apparently involves the element of universality, something found in all great literature. Oedipus, I might remind you, had trouble with his father, and Hamlet had trouble with his stepfather, while Romeo and Juliet, a pair of really unbalanced teen-agers, had trouble with everybody.

At the risk of losing literary status, and perhaps failing to get onto the required reading list, I am going to be more restrained than Sophocles and Shakespeare. The teen-agers I write about will not entertain the reader by killing their fathers, marrying their mothers, stabbing everybody in sight, or tearing their eyes out of their sockets in moments of pique. This may keep me from becoming a Great Author, but I simply haven't the stomach for writ-

ing about such far-out types. The close-in ones are enough for me.

Many who have written about teen-agers have been M.D.s, or at least Ed.D.s. At first blush—and I confess to having blushed about this more than once —my own graduate work in English Philology would appear inadequate and inappropriate for the present task. Yet I have found it extremely useful. Without my study of Anglo-Saxon, Middle English dialects, Gothic, Old Norse, and the Indo-European vowel system, I would be far more baffled than I am by the primitive means of communication which passes for language among present-day teen-agers. What to the untrained ear is nothing more than a series of meaningless grunts, with a barely detectable pattern of gutturals and sibilants, is to the expert philologist (which I am not) a fascinating reversion to prerecorded speech, slightly flavored by pig Latin.

"Pormesum war," my son says to my daughter, across the dinner table.

"Goan geddid. Yucan geddid swellas icansilly," my daughter replies, and I set to work at once translating this tantalizing bit of repartee.

In a matter of minutes, after thumbing—and forefingering—my book of *Teenese Words and Phrases,* I come up with a rough but adequate translation. "Pour me some water" is English for what my son said. And "Go on, get it. You can get it as well as I can, silly" is a free rendering of my daughter's response.

"Noneeduv beanrudaboudid," I put in, which is Teenese for "No need of being rude about it." I know only a few phrases, and my pronunciation is none too good, but my youngsters are impressed. If they want to cut me out of the conversation completely, they will have to speak more rapidly, as they can easily do.

So I was once a teen-ager, and I have some knowledge of philology. But my most valuable qualification I have saved for the last. I am nearing the end of two terms, fortunately served almost concurrently, as the parent of teen-agers. What I mean by this is that my son and daughter, slightly less than two years apart in age, either have reached or are within a year of reaching the chronological end of teen age. How many more years it will be until they are adults actually as well as chronologically is anyone's guess. Some of my own guesses might sound a little extreme, so I shall not mention them.

Actually, it's all a deception:

You parents who think that your children will grow
    More easy to handle some day,
More earnest and willing, the more things they know,
    Are wrong, I am sorry to say.

As children grow older, the change is inclined,
    As it happens, to be the reverse:
When they're old enough to know better, you'll find
    They're old enough to know worse.

The past several years I have studied my two teen-agers—and their incredible friends—as dispassionately and scientifically as possible, allowing for a tendency to headaches and an occasional blind rage. If I have said "my" teen-agers when I should have said "our," I know my wife will forgive me, because I am concerned chiefly with their objectionable qualities, and these, my wife is quick to admit, were inherited from my side of the family.

These, then, are my qualifications. I would display not only my credentials but my scars, were not these mostly on my psyche, which it would be hard for anyone to get a good look at, even if I took off my shirt.

Come to think of it, my shirt is already off. My son borrowed it and left me his—the one with the hole burnt in the shirttail. How it got there, since my son stopped playing with matches several years ago, I can't figure out. He tells me it was caused when someone at school tried to give him a hotfoot and, apparently, missed by about a yard. This is as plausible as most of his explanations, so I am inclined to believe him.

Now, holding onto your hat—and your shirt— press forward with me, with gun and camera, into Darkest Adolescence.

I: Remember, they are sick

Adolescence is a disease. It may not be listed in the medical books as such, but that is only because doctors are embarrassed to be reminded of something in the presence of which they are so helpless. Like the common cold, there is no cure for it. Unlike the common cold, nothing can be prescribed, such as aspirin, which will give the patient temporary relief. The most that can be done is to give aspirin, along with a shot of whiskey, to those who are unlucky enough to have come in contact with the victim.

"Doctor," a distraught parent shouts into the phone, "Tommy has it bad."

"Has what?" the doctor asks, momentarily forgetting that he is the one who gets paid for a diagnosis.

"I don't know, but he's never been like this before. You'd better come right over."

The doctor comes as quickly as he can. Since he lives only a few blocks away, he is there, with his little black bag, within a couple of hours.

"Let me see your tongue," he tells the poor boy, though as soon as he glimpses that mottled face and encounters that vacant stare, he knows what the trouble is. Having asked to see his tongue, he has to go through with it and give the thing a professional look. Thanks to his medical training and clinical experience, the sight makes him only slightly queasy.

"Take two of these at bedtime," he says, tapping some white pills into a small envelope on which he writes the directions. "No, these aren't for Tommy, they're for you. They'll help you sleep. You're going to need all your strength, because what Tommy's got will probably last five or six years."

And then the doctor is gone, leaving behind a couple of used tongue depressors and the faint odor of formaldehyde.

Happily, the disease is not contagious. Adolescents do not give adolescence to their parents, even when they drink from the same glass or cough right into their faces. No doubt the reason for this is that adolescence, like chickenpox and mumps, is a disease that you get only once, after which you build up an immunity. It is also like chickenpox and mumps in that you usually get it early in life, and it goes harder with you if you come down with it after you are forty or so.

This rarely happens, but now and then one comes upon a case of adolescence in middle age. Such an unfortunate occurrence is usually explained by the patient's having had an extremely mild case in childhood, which failed to develop the necessary immunity. Or it may be a case that never completely ran its course but lay dormant, like diabetes or tuberculosis, ready to reappear whenever resistance was low.

Most middle-aged adolescents, however, are those who initially were struck so hard that they never recovered. They went on living, because adolescence is seldom fatal, but they were unable to throw off the disease, which lasted thirty, forty, or fifty years. I know a man forty-three years old who since he was thirteen has never been free of the disease one day in his life. He wears bright-colored vests and drives a hot rod and yells himself hoarse at the high school football games and drinks too much and dances the teen-age dances and uses the current teen-age slang. His few remaining friends have considerately stopped asking, "Aren't you ever going to grow up?" Anyhow, they know he never will.

But normally the first stages of adolescence set in at about twelve or thirteen, and the terms "adolescent" and "teen-ager" are therefore interchangeable. Often, however, adolescence begins to show itself at ten or eleven, especially in that peculiarly obnoxious creature, the precocious child (*dementia praecox,* or precocious little demon). By beginning adolescence two or three years earlier, such a child goes through just that many more years of it, meanwhile brazenly pretending to have skipped adolescence entirely.

It does no good whatsoever to discover the disease early, except to ease your mind about its being what it is. At the same time it may depress you to realize that your child has something that will drag on for years and years and not be over in a few weeks, like scarlet fever or pneumonia.

As for how it is detected, you might look for one or more of the following symptoms:

1. A sudden listlessness and lack of ambition, in some instances accompanied by complete inability to perform such everyday tasks as getting out of bed in the morning.

2. In sharp contrast, and the sort of thing that makes diagnosis difficult, the male may have a sudden desire to lift heavy objects, such as bar bells, so long as the lifting serves no useful purpose to society.

3. Periods of forgetfulness and mental lapse bordering on amnesia, especially regarding anything important to another member of the family, for instance the fact that an urgent telephone call was to be returned as soon as possible. It might be expressed this way:

> A mind? Yes, he
> Has one of those.
> It comes, however,
> And it goes.

> And if, when it
> Is called upon,
> It mostly happens
> To be gone,

> Don't fret, don't shout,
> Don't curse the lack.
> Just wait a while—
> It will be back.

Informal diagnosis by a member of the family, without benefit of X rays or laboratory tests, is usually adequate. A thermometer thrust into the mouth will probably come out registering 98.6°, and all that may be achieved is the discovery that there are nicotine stains on the lower teeth and that there is a remarkable depression in the roof of the mouth where a wad of gum may be stored without interfering with speech.

A friend of mine, not knowing the above, took his young son to the doctor. Confident that there was something seriously wrong, he requested a complete physical and mental examination. Everything went easily enough, and the doctor thought he had a routine case, until he placed his stethoscope to the boy's lungs and started to listen. There was an odd humming noise.

"Strange," the doctor said, not believing his ears, in which he had previously trusted implicitly. "Breathe deeply, Sonny," he directed his patient, and listened intently again, a puzzled look on his face.

The doctor was a thorough, scientific sort of fellow, and he eventually noticed that the humming noise was made only when the boy was exhaling. Now he was on the right track, and soon he was convinced that the humming noise was—a humming noise. Afflicted with nothing more than a severe case of adolescence, it turned out that the boy was merely humming a popular tune. This humming is a fairly common symptom of advanced adolescence, when a craving for music makes it necessary to hum a tune during the short periods when separated from a radio or record player. Otherwise, there is that dreadful quiet which a teen-ager can endure only about as long as he can hold his breath.

As for treatment of the disease, it would be a mistake to put the adolescent in bed, having had

such a time getting him out of it. He might stay there indefinitely, getting up only when necessary to go to the bathroom or to the refrigerator. Nor is there any use dosing him with sulfa, penicillin, aureomycin, or cortisone.

Once it is certain a child has adolescence, should you tell him? Or, if you lack the courage, should you ask the doctor to do so? No. Not knowing the seriousness of his illness, not knowing all that lies ahead of him, he will think you unduly alarmed.

"Get hold of yourself," he will say, as you brush away the tears and try to keep your lower lip from trembling too noticeably. "I'll live through it."

Maybe he will, you think to yourself. But will *we?*

The wise parent will fight back the impulse to tell the teen-ager what is the matter with him. Not only will adolescents never admit they are adolescents (in this respect, as in so many others, resembling mental patients), but they resent having the term applied to them. Call them "stupid fool" or "nitwit" or "nincompoop" (which they probably wouldn't understand, anyhow, and would be too lazy to look up), but never, especially in a scornful tone of voice, "adolescent." An adolescent too often called an adolescent may do something drastic, such as run away from home. So you should be careful with the word, unless you have been looking for a way to get the child to move out.

In short, adolescents, however badly stricken, are not only beyond help but do not wish help, especially from their parents. Parents of their friends are something else again.

"Jeanne's mother and father understand me," my teen-age daughter is always saying, "even if you don't."

The interesting thing is that Jeanne's mother and father, who do indeed understand my daughter, don't understand Jeanne. We do. So when my daughter is un-understood by us, she goes to Jeanne's house, and when Jeanne is un-understood by her parents, she comes to ours. It is a fine system, a kind of two-way Lend-Lease. Sometimes our daughter and theirs, each headed for the other's house, pass a few blocks away, at mid-point. The only trouble is that the teen-age girl in our house a large part of the time is not our daughter but Jeanne, and the one who seems to be a regular member of the other household is not Jeanne but our daughter. Guests are understandably bewildered, and we grow tired of explaining. The fact that the two girls wear identical clothes and hairdos adds to the confusion. Sometimes we are not sure ourselves.

But I have been using my daughter as an example too much. There is also my son, about whom it might be said:

> Our son does little, now, but grow,
> And that he does a lot.
> He's "shooting up," we say, and so
> No wonder we are shot.

Yes, adolescents are sick, and not to be held accountable for their actions. Despite what some old-fashioned penologists say, it would be unfair to put them away for a few years in a maximum-security prison. It would not only be unfair but, what is more important, it would be illegal, and you could wind up in prison yourself. You might enjoy the peace and quiet, at that.

"There ought to be a law," I have heard some parents mutter, but it was only wishful thinking. If such a law were passed, it would promptly be declared unconstitutional by some soft-hearted judge, in all likelihood a bachelor.

As of now, there is nothing to do about adolescence but let it run its course, wear itself out. There are those who optimistically take hope in the advance of science in the parallel fields of poliomyelitis, diabetes, and schizophrenia. Indeed, there may in time be not only tuberculosis stamps but adolescence stamps, and the Cancer Fund may be matched by the Adolescence Fund, aimed at supplying adequate resources for research that may lead to a scientific breakthrough. Should such a fund drive get underway, hundreds of thousands of volunteer workers stand ready to canvass every home in the land, taking with them stickers bearing such forthright, crusading slogans as "Stamp Out Adolescence" and "We Gave."

Some day a Dr. Salk will probably come along with a vaccine for adolescence. If so, the only question will be which Nobel Prize he should get—the one for medicine or the one for peace.

But until then, my advice to parents of teen-agers is to remember that these young people are sick. Be kind. Visit them only during visiting hours and only when bearing gifts of candy, clothing, electronic gadgets, and money—especially money.

As for corporal punishment, you wouldn't hit an invalid, would you?

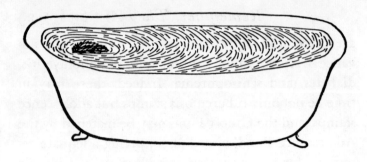

II: The bathroom

When one of my teen-agers is around the house somewhere, but not in sight, I always try the bathroom. If the door is locked, I know I am on the right track.

"Are you in there?" I cry. Or, this being pretty obvious, "When are you coming out?"

If there is no response, I rattle the doorknob and pound with my fist. If I achieve nothing else, by banging the door hard enough and long enough I may toughen the skin on my knuckles. Parents who are skilled in the Japanese art of *karate* can, I suppose, drive their fist through the ordinary door with one determined blow, and this must be pretty impressive.

Occasionally when I ask, "Are you in there?" I get some such informative reply as "No." The answer to "When are you coming out?" is usually "Just a minute," which is meant to be encouraging. However, I happen to know that the teen-ager's minute has little relationship to sixty seconds, and that such a unit of time is better checked with a calendar than with a watch.

In short, when an adolescent goes into the bathroom he goes there to stay. It does no good to raise your voice, to plead, or to threaten. Even the note of urgency in such a heartrending appeal as "I've *got* to get in there right away!" will have no effect. The adolescent is not heartless. He knows that, in event of an emergency, there is always the next-door neighbor's bathroom. Or the public lavatory downtown.

Parents have been known to become frantic about the long sojourn, bordering upon permanent residence, of a teen-ager in the bathroom. With no response to questions, and no sound detectable to an ear placed like a stethoscope against the door, they have concluded that the youngster has fallen from the window and have rushed outside, carrying a sheet to throw over the crumpled body.

I remember the time my wife and I stood close to our bathroom door, fairly certain that our son was inside but hearing no sound.

"Do you suppose he scalded himself to death in the shower?" my wife wondered aloud. She has a lively imagination and could picture his prostrate form behind the shower curtain.

"I doubt it," I said. "The water would still be running, unless he was able to turn the knob before he passed out."

"Then maybe he drowned in the tub," my wife said.

"Or electrocuted himself," I put in helpfully, "trying to listen to the radio in the bathtub."

But our son eventually emerged—alive, unhurt, and without explanation. The only casualty was a little skin off my knuckles from all that knocking, and a slight hoarseness.

At an earlier age our son, like any red-blooded youngster, would not have been in the bathroom, despite the locked door. He would have climbed out the window and shinnied up the drainpipe to the roof, imagining himself a mountain climber venturing up the last perilous escarpment to the top of Everest. But now he is too old for this sort of adventuring. He lacks both the imagination and the energy, especially the energy.

What, you might ask—and I don't blame you—does an adolescent do, hour after hour, in the bathroom?

I can only guess, because I have never stooped, physically or morally, to peek through the keyhole. (Besides, I know I would see nothing, with the key in it.) My guess is that the time-consuming activity in some way has to do with preoccupation with self, and the chances are that the focus of this activity is the mirror on the medicine chest.

In this connection, let me get off my own chest the following heartfelt lines:

> My teen-age son and daughter
>> Are thoughtful little elves.
> They think and think and think and think
>> And think about themselves.

A mirror in any part of the house has a magnetic quality that powerfully attracts and holds the adolescent, whether male or female. If the teen-ager does little deep thinking, in front of a mirror he at least reflects.

Various mirrors have various appeals. For instance, the full-length mirror in the bedroom or hall is especially useful when action and movement are involved: twirling a full skirt, dancing with an invisible partner—who always follows beautifully—practicing serves and overhead smashes, or bulging the biceps. If two or three mirrors can be so arranged that there is simultaneous viewing of the front, side, and rear, there can be careful analysis of the triply reflected posture, which may encourage flexing of pectoral muscles or insertion of additional foam rubber in the small-size bra. Boys and girls seem almost equally interested in chest expansion.

Of all the mirrors in the house, the one in the

bathroom has the most magnetism. It will pull an adolescent from the basement, the garage, or even the dining room, and hold him, nose almost against the glass, for an incredible period. Though I have not myself beheld the mysterious rites, I have heard a number of almost unbelievable tales from parents who either have peeked or possess an inventive imagination.

One of the things mirror-watchers do, I am told, is to jab repeatedly at the eyes with a pointed steel instrument, as if intent on blindness self-inflicted.

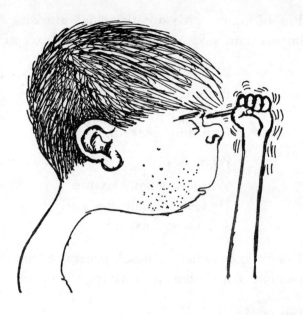

Actually the point of impact is just above the eyes, and what the adolescent is doing is plucking eyebrows—not being content to look like an aborigine with one solid line of scraggly black hair from temple to temple.

Plucking eyebrows, you will protest, is something done only by girls. But if you think this, you are unfamiliar with the male ego. The only difference between boys and girls in this regard is that boys are more careful not to let it appear that there has been any tampering with nature.

But of course girls are the chief pluckers and primpers, and my own daughter is no exception:

> Peering above,
> Probing beneath,
> Curling her lashes,
> Brushing her teeth,
>
> Daubing her face
> With every new mixture,
> My teen-age daughter's
> A bathroom fixture.

I don't know whether this is general or not, but my daughter has a horror of having anyone else use her towel.

"Oh, look what you've done!" she said to me once, as she came into the bathroom just as I was leaving. Dismay and disgust were written all over her face, in capital letters.

"Have I done something wrong?" I asked in all innocence.

"You used my towel," she said, and I thought she was going to cry.

"I only touched the corner of it," I said. "I thought it was mine. And my hands were clean. I had just washed them."

"You're disgusting," she said, and she plucked the towel from the rack, holding it cautiously by the corner—the corner I had not used—and dropped it into the hamper. A shudder went through her, as if she had been handling a snake.

"I'm sorry," I said, though I really wasn't.

"Don't you ever do that again," she said, and I never did—not when my own towel was handy and I could remember which one it was.

Teen-agers can be awfully fastidious about some things, and considering how sloppy they are generally, I should be glad, even when I am treated like a leper.

But let us return to our consideration of what they do, all that time, in the bathroom. Besides tweezer work, another thing that occupies them, I am told, is looking at the back of the head and the profile, with the help of a hand mirror. This does not take in all of the areas included in a full-length mirror, but it accommodates the part most often seen by the public. Moreover, it permits pinpoint specialization—one square inch at a time, even pore by pore.

They also make sundry grimaces for the purpose of demonstrating facial mobility, deepening dimples, and creating faint resemblances to stars of stage and screen. These facial contortions include pressing the nose up, down, and sideways, to see how much better it would look if it were bobbed or uptilted. After one of these sessions, it is frequently decided to put aside a certain portion of the weekly allowance for plastic surgery. Interestingly, I have it from a usually reliable source that the adolescent of today no longer practices wiggling his ears in front of the mirror, this entrancing exercise of my own youth now being considered old hat, or old ears.

Our bathroom mirror has a bubble in it, about nose high. I can imagine the happy hours my son and daughter spend in front of it, moving slightly up and down and right and left, and smearing the nose all over the face. The reason I can imagine this is that I get such a kick out of doing it myself. Sometimes I do it while shaving—and get so fascinated that I cut a hunk out of my chin.

But an adolescent needs no defect in the glass to hold him transfixed, staring into the mirror. It may be self-hypnosis, or it may be more akin to self-adoration. One is reminded of the Greek myth of Narcissus, who fell in love with his reflection in a pool, never having seen anything so beautiful. After admiring himself for a few years, he fell into the pool and became a flower. This much is sure about Narcissus: he was an adolescent.

For some odd reason, adults fail to comprehend what is so attractive to an adolescent about his face. How could he possibly stand there looking at it hour after hour? Face-watching seems to be his chief occupation and, if this continues, will be his life work. Not until he starts going steady will there be another face at which he can gaze for so long and with such rapture.

It is best, if you have the will power—and other bathroom facilities—to leave the adolescent undisturbed and, when he at last emerges, make no sarcastic remarks. For emerge he will, having temporarily had enough of his face or having begun to suffer hunger pangs. Instead of wondering what he has been doing all this time, show him how glad you are to have him back, and no questions asked. See as much of him as you can, and get reacquainted.

For it will not be long until he is back in the bathroom, at the same old stand.

Before leaving, with some reluctance, the subject of this chapter, let me describe one noteworthy feature of the bathroom in our house, something that binds our family together, adults and adolescents:

> We have a bathroom door that sticks.
> It will not yield to tugs or kicks.
> Once tightly closed, it will withstand
> The strength of any unskilled hand.
>
> It takes a certain pull and lift,
> Which some say is an art, a gift.
> The wrist must twist, the shoulder heave.
> You have to see it to believe.
>
> And though we have the skill, the knack,
> This isn't true of guests, alack,
> Who can't get in or (worse, no doubt)
> Get in, then think they can't get out.

III: Clothes

"Have you seen my tan gabardine slacks?" I asked my son, opening the door to his room slightly and poking my head in. I didn't go all the way in, because he was cleaning a shotgun and the muzzle was pointing directly at me.

"I think they're around here somewhere," he said, and as soon as he finished cleaning the gun he helpfully started rummaging through his closet.

"Maybe they're in one of your dresser drawers," I suggested when he seemed to be having no luck.

"No, I remember now," he said, "I have them on."

The reason I didn't recognize them, although they were my favorite slacks, was that my son had cut them off at the knees and made walking shorts of them.

"I thought you didn't want them any more," he said, when he saw my face turn ashen, as it always does when I am slightly annoyed about something. "Anyhow," he added brightly, "I saved you the twelve-fifty it would have cost for a pair of gabardine walking shorts."

"Thanks," I said, mentally subtracting twelve-fifty from twenty-five dollars, the cost of a new pair of slacks, and doubting I could ever find another pair as good as my old ones.

"You're welcome," he said, more polite than usual, and relieved because the color was coming back into my face.

"I appreciate your good intentions," I said, surprised at my self-control. "But I really would prefer them as slacks again. Maybe I can get your mother to sew them back together." Then I asked, looking around, "Where are the lower parts, from the knee down?"

Before he told me, I found out for myself. One trouser leg was lying on the floor, in good shape. The other, however, had been cut into inch-wide strips. Apparently there's nothing quite so good as tan gabardine for cleaning the barrel of a shotgun.

I shut the door quietly and tiptoed away. Fortunately, I am too much of a coward for either murder or suicide.

My son not only fools around with guns, which it is hard for me to believe, despite his assurances, are unloaded, but he lifts weights. Ever since there has been even the slightest development of his biceps, he has taken to wearing only a T shirt around the house, even in the dead of winter.

"Aren't you cold?" I ask him. It gives me goose pimples just to watch him parade around in that skin-tight T shirt when I am wearing a sweater and jacket and have just turned up the furnace.

"No," he says, hunching his shoulders to make his neck seem shorter and thicker. "Hit me in the stomach. Go on, hit me hard."

He stiffens his muscles and I give him a fairly sharp blow to the midsection. I hope I haven't hurt him, and I haven't, but I have sprained my right index finger and spend the evening soaking it in hot water and Epsom salts.

What bothers my wife about his wearing a T shirt all the time isn't the possibility of his catching cold. It's his wearing a T shirt to dinner.

"Won't you please put on a shirt and coat, or a shirt anyhow?" she begs him. "It just doesn't look right at the dinner table."

What worries her is what the neighbors will think. We have a large picture window, and our neighbors are always out walking their dog, whatever the hour or the weather. The dog doesn't need all that exercise. In fact the worn-down little dachshund could use some rest. But these people want to know what's going on. We could draw the curtains, but that gives my son claustrophobia.

At least that's what he says. Actually, he sits at the dinner table facing the window, which at night reflects almost as well as a mirror. In that T shirt, with his shoulders hunched, he is quite a physical specimen, he thinks. And our neighbors, I fear, consider us pretty low class.

While my son is content to go around in the same style of T shirt, as long as there is nothing over it to

obscure his muscles, my daughter insists upon variety. To be reduced to wearing a party dress that she wore once before, and only three months ago, would be to reach the depths of social degradation, as it would for any sensitive (normal) teen-age girl. Hester Prynne was unusual, keeping her chin up while going around, day after day, wearing the same old blouse, with a scarlet "A" embroidered on it. No wonder the other girls stared at her and whispered things like "She's in a rut" and "Doesn't she know blouses like that went out a couple of years ago?" and "Looks homemade to me." The only time a teen-age girl will be seen in the same outfit for weeks and months, and with a great big scarlet "A" to boot, is when she's wearing her boy friend's Auburn High football sweater.

It is of little consequence to our daughter whether her clothes indicate good taste in color or pattern. Or even whether they fit. (While her own boy friend's football sweater has a "C" on it, for Claremont High, instead of an "A," he is a 180-pound lineman, and on my daughter this garment looks like a knitted overcoat, which is the way it's supposed to look.) The chief requisite is that clothes be this year's style— or, better, this month's. Asked to wear an out-of-style coat because it is still nice looking and warm and has been worn only a few times, my daughter has been heard (by me) to say, "I'd rather die." She would, too.

As if there were not enough trouble caused by change of style, there is also change of mind:

> One day a child will tease for clothing
> That's viewed next day with look of loathing.
> The coat, the shirt, whatever article,
> Although it hasn't changed a particle,
> Will be considered quite unbearable,
> Unsuitable, and thus unwearable.
> And all that parents know, I find,
> About this sudden change of mind
> Is that it fills the shelves and hooks
> And helps to empty pocketbooks.

This does not mean that a teen-ager wants to be just like everybody else. He or she wants to be more like everybody else than anybody else. It is imperative that adults grasp this concept if they are to know what makes a teen-ager tick, and what to do if the ticking becomes ominous. The ideal of the teen-ager, with regard to clothes, is to be neither conspicuous, in the sense of being different, nor inconspicuous, in the sense of being unimaginatively like everyone else and therefore not noticed.

This may seem trivial to an adult, but it can be crucial to a teen-ager. There have been instances when a pair of standard yet artistically soiled corduroy trousers have been decisive in winning election to a student body office. My own daughter failed to become a cheer leader in high school because her tennis shoes lacked the mud and grass stains and the delicate patina of mold which graced the shoes of the girl who nosed her out in the balloting. Afterward, she went into seclusion for a week, claiming she had a cold but actually working on her tennis shoes with dirt, grass, and an abrasive instrument. Obviously, her political career was not ended, and she hoped to run again—in her improved tennis shoes.

Not that my daughter wears only tennis shoes, though she does most of the time. She has footwear of every conceivable type, and yet around the house she goes barefoot. Her first act, on entering the front door, is to take off her shoes, which she drops right there unless she knows of another place where they look worse. Let me put it this way:

> We've only a teen-age daughter,
> A two-legged creature indeed,
> And yet from the shoes
> She incessantly strews,
> You'd think we've a centipede.

The parent who appreciates the teen-ager's desire to dress like all the others and yet more so will avoid such a tragic mistake as my wife once made. This well-meaning but ignorant woman sent our son's sweat shirt to the laundry for what seemed to her two excellent reasons: (1) it had a catsup stain down the front and (2) it smelled, as she said in her quaint way, "to high heaven."

How was she to know that it was an antique and beautifully placed catsup stain that gave the sweat shirt exactly the desired air of casualness, and that the peculiar fragrance enabled our son to identify his sweat shirt in the school locker room even before he got inside?

Usually there is no objection to the purchase of new clothes. But the need for new clothes bears no relationship to the supply of old clothes in perfectly good condition.

"I've just *got* to have a wool skirt," our daughter said one day, a note of desperation in her voice.

"But you *have* a wool skirt, haven't you?" I asked. Her mother and I had checked her closet only the day before and had discovered that, by actual count, she had fourteen wool skirts—pleated, unpleated, pleated in front only, pleated in back only, heavy, lightweight, plaid, plain, belted, unbelted, etc.

"Yes, but I haven't a skirt to go with my green blouse," she said. It occurred to me to ask why in heck she hadn't bought a blouse to go with one of her fourteen skirts, instead of buying the green one. However, I checked myself from saying something that would not only upset my daughter but be considered by my wife an attack upon herself. The two of them frequently give me the impression that they have signed a mutual aid treaty.

Buying one article of clothing in order to require another article of clothing is a gambit passed along, mother to daughter, generation to generation—a bit of cunning against which a man has no defense.

So, in this instance, I had the sense to keep quiet. The only possible indication that I questioned my daughter's logic was the trickle of blood from my mouth caused by biting my lips.

Of course we bought her another wool skirt. My wife went with her to the store, to help pick it out, and in the process found a wool skirt for herself as well as a blouse and sweater to "go with" the skirt. In restaurants I have found that anything that "goes with" the table d'hôte dinner is included in the price, but clothes, alas, are à la carte.

A teen-ager has another reason for making purchases which is considered a clincher. "Jane (or John) has one," the youngster shrewdly says. Or, spoken in a tone of mingled irritation and condescension calculated to reduce a parent to quivering helplessness, *"Everybody* has one!" This may refer, of course, not merely to an article of clothing but to a motor scooter or a portable TV.

Once I thought I had an answer to this inane claim—a way to put down, or at least put off, my son:

> When "all my friends" have this or that
>   That's wanted by my son,
> To silence him, day after day,
> I've found I merely have to say,
>   "Name one."

This worked for a while, but eventually it failed me. The time came when I said, brusquely, "Name one," and he did. As it happened, in this instance the item was a Thunderbird. You can never be sure when the John your son is palling around with is John D. Rockefeller IV.

But I am not one to give up without a fight. To wriggle out of such an embarrassing and potentially expensive situation as this, I have discovered a few sly maneuvers which I pass along to perplexed parents:

——Explain at length, preferably at a blackboard, the superior economic status of Jane's (or John's) father. If this elicits such questions as "Then why don't you earn more? Aren't you as smart as he is?" employ diversionary tactics, perhaps tossing in a statement like "What you need is to learn the value of a dollar." (You will be lucky if you are not asked what the value of a dollar is. When you last checked, it was around thirty-nine cents.)

——Suggest buying something cheaper which everyone else also has, such as a pair of shoestrings with luminous ends, to facilitate putting on shoes in the dark. This will almost certainly be rejected, but it will gain a little time to think, and there is always the chance that the doorbell will ring or someone will telephone and the whole thing will be forgotten, though not for long.

——Call up Jane's father and John's father—yes, call up *everybody's* father—and check on the accuracy of the statement. If you find even one household which does not possess the article in question, confront your teen-ager with the results of your poll. "See, you were wrong," you can say, pointing to the list of names and notations. "George Gunderson doesn't have a tennis court, and that makes two of you." Your teen-ager will probably then say, "Well, I meant *almost* everybody. And besides, you don't want people to think you're as stingy as old Mr. Gunderson, do you?" If you hold your ground, you might start a trend, and fathers everywhere will bless you. But you probably won't.

——Call a meeting of all the parents in the neighborhood and form an association. Name it something unusual, like P.T.A. (Parents of Teen-Agers), and elect a President, several Vice-Presidents, a Secretary, and a Treasurer. Have the members swear a solemn oath, to be repeated as a pledge of allegiance at each meeting: "I solemnly swear not to be pushed into buying any article" (not even something as common-place as a pair of rhinoceros-hide shoes with minia-ture tusks on the toe) "on the grounds that 'every-body has one,' without permission from the Execu-tive Committee, so help me God." Any parent who makes an unauthorized purchase will, in addition to the regular dues, pay a fine equal to the cost of the item. Money collected from dues and fines will be used for a worthwhile neighborhood project, such as a sound-proof bomb shelter, where parents can seek refuge when the record player is going full blast.

——One final suggestion: give in, and buy such clothing as your teen-ager demands. Think how happy this will make not only your youngster but the local merchants, and how this will stimulate the economy and lead to a reduction in the national debt, even as your own increases. You may, indeed, be named Parent of the Year by the Chamber of Com-merce, and presented with a monogrammed leather case in which to carry your checkbook.

Or maybe you would prefer an extra-large, Easy-Open billfold, from which currency can be extracted in a jiffy. Its usefulness will be indicated by the fol-lowing:

> My teen-age son is in a dash,
> He hits me up, and quick, for cash.
> He asks, he's off, he's never slow.
> With him it's always touch and go.

True, you can always wear the faddish clothes of which your teen-ager has tired. You will not only save money but gain an enviable reputation for wearing jaunty, youthful outfits—slash pockets, skin-tight trousers—and will stand out in any group of middle-aged persons. You may not only stand out but, in those tight trousers, bulge out.

Naturally, if you are going to wear discards, you must keep yourself the same weight and height as your teen-ager, who has a tendency to grow taller as you grow broader. How you are to manage this is your problem, not mine.

IV: Around the house

Sunday morning, the only morning when I might stay in bed after 7:00 A.M., is also my only time to do the yard work and wash the car. Perhaps I shouldn't be so selfish, but I find it a little hard to pull weeds and rake the leaves out of a rocky flower bed, knowing that my muscular son is lifting weights in the room above. I hope I am not being ill-tempered when I rattle the stones unnecessarily and now and then toss one at the window screen.

My feelings on the subject are so strong that on occasion I have waxed lyrical. One fine summer day I took my pen in my calloused hand and expressed myself thusly:

54

Through years of waiting, long and tough,
  I've watched the growing brawn.
At last the lad is strong enough
  To mow and edge the lawn.

I've dreamed of lying in the shade
  With not the slightest stirring,
While he (as I sip lemonade)
  Would keep the mower whirring.

Well, here I lie, stretched out full length,
  Beside my faithful pup, yet.
I've mowed, and now I'm gaining strength—
  My son? He isn't up yet.

But I must not be too hard on the boy. When it comes to washing the car, one of the jobs I dislike most, he is a real help.

You see, I hate to work alone, without anyone to sympathize with me or urge me on. And when I wash the car, my son is touchingly faithful about keeping me company and giving me helpful hints.

"You missed a spot on the hood," he says, and I discover the place and rub it extra hard.

"How does it look now?" I ask, hopeful of coming up to his exacting standards.

"Pretty good, Dad," he says, "but you're going to use some chrome polish on the bumpers, aren't you?"

As a matter of fact I wasn't, because I had polished the bumpers the Sunday before, and I thought they could go for another week.

"Of course," I say, not wishing him to think me slapdash or lazy. For a moment I consider asking him to go into the house and get me the can of polish and a fresh rag, but he looks so comfortable, sitting in that contour chair I helped him carry out to the front lawn, that I decide not to disturb him. Besides, he might go for the polish and rag and not come back. And, as I have said, I like company while I work.

So I polish the bumpers and go over the windows once more, to catch a few streaks I had missed. I finish none too soon. When I look up, I see my son sitting at the wheel, his hand on the ignition key.

"That's good enough, Dad," he says, starting the motor. "I've got to go see John." John is his best friend, and he hasn't seen him for a period of several hours.

As he drives off, carefully hitting a mud puddle, I roll up the hose and pick up the sponge, rags, bucket, broom, and other impedimenta of car washing. The contour chair is too heavy for me to carry into the house by myself, but my wife will help me.

It would add to my pleasure as a car washer if my daughter were also in the gallery, lending her presence and her advice. But if this is the usual Sunday morning, I must get along without her. She is enjoying a well-deserved late-morning sleep, worn out by a Saturday afternoon and evening which included waving a pompon incessantly throughout The Big Game, simultaneously screaming, biting her fingernails, patting her hair back into place, and freshening her lipstick—all this followed by The Big Dance. While she rests, her mother picks up coats, sweaters, a megaphone, a program, candy wrappers, popcorn, and bobby pins, so that she can make her way into the kitchen to prepare dinner.

As a matter of fact, my daughter has ways of wearing herself out without going to a football game or even going outdoors. Her specialty is this amazing performance, to be observed daily:

> My teen-age daughter flops and falls
> And flips and slips and slumps and sprawls
> And twists and twines and coils and loops
> And writhes and jerks and drapes and droops.
> Is this a workout in the gym?
> Does she have fits? Is it a whim?
> No, don't be frightened, please don't stare.
> She's merely "sitting" in a chair.

Farmers, I know, get a full day's work out of their children, even when they are teen-agers. In fact, I am told that farmers have large families in order to get

free labor. What other reason could there possibly be? But most of us are city dwellers, and household chores in a city or suburb somehow lack the challenge of fetching eggs from the hen house and pouring slops into the pig trough.

The only livestock in our house is a dog, a cat, and a canary. Washing a dog is fun only the first time—and not even then for the dog—while cleaning up after a sick cat or changing the paper in the canary's cage just doesn't make a teen-ager feel he is doing something creative, or essential to the nation's economy.

However, it would seem possible to send a youth to the supermarket for ready-cut, ready-wrapped bacon, inasmuch as he has been spared the rigors of pig-slopping, especially on a sloppy day.

"Run up to the store and get two pounds of bacon," my wife told our son the other day. "And be sure to get the kind that's on sale." She pressed a ten-dollar bill into his sweaty hand and reminded him to bring back the change.

It is three blocks to the neighborhood store, and you would think the lad could get there and back in a few minutes. In this instance, which was about average, our son sauntered into the kitchen an hour later with: (1) one pound of bacon instead of two, and not the kind on sale, and (2) a paperback edition of Shakespeare, apparently as a result of a train of thought started by the word bacon. My wife was so upset about his getting the regular bacon instead of the kind on sale, a difference of four cents a pound, that she forgot to ask him for the change. When she remembered, the next day, it was too late.

"Oh, *that* ten dollars," he shrugged.

"Yes, *that* ten dollars," my wife said. There was a spark of hope in her voice, because this time, for a wonder, he wasn't insisting it was only a dollar bill.

"I remember now," he said. "I got the change, all right, and I know exactly where I put it."

"Well, go get it," my wife said.

"I put it on a pile of magazines while I was looking at the paperbacks," he said, "and it probably isn't there now."

It wasn't.

Discouraging as all this appears, there is a large amount of energy in that ungainly body, and a trace of intelligence behind that vacant stare. Harnessing these, without actually using reins and a bit, is the problem. I have a few ideas which, since they have done me no good, I pass along.

A suggestion for city dwellers is to develop more interesting chores, taking a fly-specked leaf out of the farm family's book. If zoning laws and city ordinances permit, chickens, cows, and pigs might be established in the back yard, and the front lawn might be sown in wheat. A red-blooded young man who scorns a lawn mower might delight in cutting a swath through a wheat field with a medium-size combine. Nor would he find it too taxing, since two or three swaths would do the job.

I can imagine my son coming in after cutting the front forty (feet). He would splash water over his head at the pump, which we had installed in place of the electric washer on the back porch, and clump into the kitchen, snapping his galluses the way they do on *Wagon Train*.

"Looks like a mighty fine crop, Paw," he would say, "if'n we kin git it in 'fore it rains."

But in some of the snootier residential sections a neighbor might not take kindly to the smell of the pigs and the noise of the thresher. This could lead to litigation, a spite fence, even a rock through the window.

Also, if chores became too fascinating it might be hard to get a youngster to leave them and come to dinner. Just try to drag a boy into the house when he is out in the garage, tinkering with the tractor. Not that it is easy to get his attention under any circumstances:

> A patient parent, I don't mean
>   To speak too sternly, heatedly.
> My children come when they are called,
> Provided only that they're called
>   Repeatedly.

Should you be compelled to assign the same old monotonous and unexciting tasks—dusting, dish-washing, floor waxing, car polishing—there is always the possibility of making the work more attractive by *paying* for it.

"My son makes me pay through the nose," a friend told me, and I shuddered at the condition of his nasal passages and was grateful that my son made no such unnatural demands.

Most teen-agers will wash the dishes with a fair amount of gusto (a new kind of detergent) for as little as a dollar a dish, seventy-five cents each for knives, forks, and spoons. I have found that my son, who has not learned the value of a dollar, will do a very respectable job of waxing the floor of one room for a thousand pennies. He may or may not realize

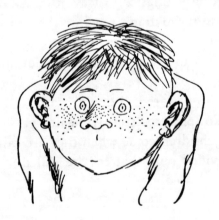

that this is only ten dollars. The way he looks at it, he can weigh himself on the scales downtown, in front of the drug store, every day for three years.

The money, after all, stays in the family. It's just taking it out of one pocket and putting it into another. Or like robbing Peter to pay Paul. The only thing is—well, I'd like to be Paul just once.

Be glad they have not yet formed a Teensters' Union. How would you like to be picketed by your own son and daughter, bearing signs reading "Unfair to Their Own Flesh and Blood," "My Father Is a Miser," and "Don't Enter Unless You Are Delivering a Bill"? Or think of a lockout, when you can't get into your own house—and not just because someone has hidden the key in a different place—or a slowdown, when your children work slower than usual, though this may be hard to imagine.

Another suggestion is this: Get your teen-ager a job with a neighbor. Teen-agers who object to sweeping the back porch for their parents, no matter at what excessive wage, will sweep the whole house and beat the rugs for someone else for a pittance. Merely crossing the property line between your house and the house next door somehow works a miracle. Whereas you cannot utter a word of criticism about a job poorly done, your neighbor can give your teen-ager a tongue lashing for having left a small spot on a window, and your wide-eyed offspring will come home, having had to work an extra half-hour for nothing, with the news that "Mr. Willoughby is a great guy. He used to be a sergeant in the Army."

Of course, if Mr. Willoughby employs your son, you in all fairness must employ his—and there is a good chance that yours is a strapping fellow, capable of lifting one end of a piano, while Mr. Willoughby's is a puny kid whom you would be ashamed to ask to lift an empty wastebasket.

There are some parents, I understand, who expect no help from their teen-agers. They have one important advantage over the others: they are never disappointed.

V: School

One of the best places to study teen-agers, I have found, is at the local high school. Occasionally I drop by at the noon hour, when the inmates emerge, and take an incredulous look. I go there partly to study the species and partly because I feel so good when I leave.

High schools are much bigger than when I was a boy, and high school boys are much bigger, too. The few times I have been inside a high school building I have felt small and frightened as I tiptoed down the long high school corridors, amidst the long high school boys. It made me understand how Gulliver felt in Brobdingnag, the land of the giants, except that the Brobdingnagians were more friendly.

On one of my visits I was heartened to see a dwarf about my size. He could not have been more than five feet ten. A warmth of fellow-feeling swept over me, and I went up to him and stuck out my hand. I wanted to throw my arms around him, but he might have thought me emotional.

"How do you do," I said, smiling attractively.

Only then did I notice he had a knife in his hand. As I spoke to him he dropped to his knees, with the knife outthrust, the blade gleaming under the corridor lights.

It was a tense moment, and I thought of throwing myself at the mercy of the nearest giant, who at least seemed to be unarmed, until I saw this dwarf start to scrape a spot on the floor with his knife. My fright left me and my feeling of comradeship returned, for I now noticed the man's mop and pail against the wall. He was the janitor (pardon me, the custodian), and he was scraping a wad of gum from the floor.

I wanted to drop to my knees beside him, but I had no knife. Also, I feared being trampled by the towering youths as they hastened down the hallway. Or a book might be dropped on me by a passing seven-footer. For they all carried books—hard, shiny volumes that looked as though they had never been opened. I edged my way toward the wall, out of the

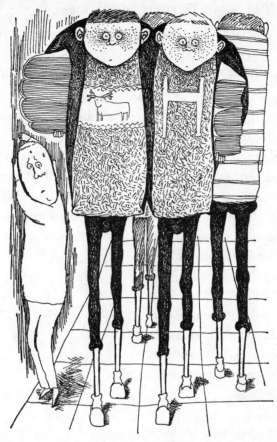

traffic flow, and inched onward to the front door and outside. It was a narrow escape.

I am full of admiration for high school teachers, who bravely enter these labyrinthine buildings and mingle with the creatures inside. There must be an easier way of making a living, such as poking at lions with a kitchen chair or being shot out of a cannon.

Teen-agers are sentenced to high school by their parents. High school, you see, takes hours and hours out of the time that might otherwise, and far more profitably, be spent at the beach or at a bowling alley or listening to records in a record shop or watching a drag race or sitting in a car, talking.

And what talking. They say the art of conversation is dead, and it may be, among adults. But once I edged up close enough to two teen-age boys, slumped over in the front seat of a car (at first I thought they had been in an accident, and were unconscious), to hear this lively interchange:

"Hey."

"Huh?"

"Whaddaya wanta do?"

"I dunno. Whaddaya wanta do?"

"I dunno."

(Silence of several minutes.)

"Hey."

"Huh?"

"Whaddayasay we go to Rusty's?"

"Unh unh."

"Whaddaya say we go to Dave's?"

"Unh unh."

(Silence of several minutes.)

"Whaddaya wanta do?"

"I dunno. Whaddaya wanta do?"

"Whaddayasay we go to Al's?"

"What for?"

"Mary might be there."

"Think so?"

"Yeah."

"Whydaya think so?"

"She kinda likes Al."

"Think so?"

"Yeah."

(Silence of several minutes.)

"Lesgo to Al's."

High school interrupts good, man-to-man talk like this and uses up valuable time that might be spent at Al's house, watching TV and watching Al watch Mary. The only teen-agers who escape high school are the few lucky ones who have understanding parents who let them get married or go to work or join the Navy.

But high school is not a total loss to young people. They get a few things out of it. One, if they are lucky, is election to an important office, such as assistant song leader. If not elected, they may be nominated for such an office, get honoroble mention, or be considered good material for another year. This feeds the ego, and the ego of a teen-ager is always hungry.

Another thing they salvage from those high school years is memorabilia, some of which is rather memorabilious, such as class sweaters that quickly sag to the knees, class rings that are the wrong size and either cut off the circulation or are held on with adhesive tape, and yearbooks with clever comments penned under pictures, such as "Nice knowing you," "Have fun," and "Hi!"

A few other benefits of a high school education are a steady boy friend—or girl friend—and several unsteady ones, a bill for laboratory breakage, and a stubborn case of athlete's foot.

At high schools there is always a Mr. Holsingbeck, the Principal, who is to be kept away from. Little do terrified students realize how Mr. Holsingbeck stammers and shakes in the presence of Mr. Dillsworth, the Superintendent, who in turn stands with bowed head in the presence of the Board of Education. A student, if he is fortunate, sees the Principal only at the opening ceremonies and graduation, when he can be heard over all the others in the "Star-Spangled Banner" and the Flag Salute, not because he is the most patriotic, but because he is closest to the microphone.

Another important personage is Miss Rumplemeyer, the Counselor of Students, who is hard outside but soft inside, like an uncooked egg. She gets tears in her eyes and blows her nose on an undersized, inadequate handkerchief when she has to tell a teen-ager that he or she is in trouble, which is something the teen-ager already knows.

Miss Rumplemeyer is rumored to have come close to marrying. According to one story, she could have married Clark Gable, who was mad about her, but she turned him down. According to another, she was engaged to a dashing young officer in some war or other (World War I or the Boer War or the Spanish–American War), who was reported missing in action but may still be alive, and she keeps a light on all night on her front porch, just in case. There are many other stories about Miss Rumplemeyer's passionate past, all of which the students believe. Some adults, who have seen Miss Rumplemeyer, are skeptical.

And then there is the Coach, "Beefy" Boyd, who is carried on the shoulders of the students in a victory parade or hanged in effigy, depending on how the game with Southside High comes out. The Coach looms much more important than either the Principal or the Counselor of Students, and it comes as something of a shock to a teen-ager when good old "Beefy," after five successful seasons, including winning the All-Conference and the Inter-Sectional, leaves his wife and three children and runs off with the new gym teacher, the one with the tiny waist who wears a tight sweater and no bra, as you can tell when she jumps up and down, leading calisthenics. Such things are remembered much longer than the date of the Boston Tea Party or who was Vice-President under William Henry Harrison.

My own son and daughter seem to have got the most, during their high school years, from the School Cafeteria, where they could choose their food, as they could not at home, where we do not publish our menu the day before.

"Did you have a good lunch?" my wife asked our son one evening, when he left his salad and pot roast and mashed potatoes and string beans virtually untouched, merely messing them up sufficiently to disqualify them for leftovers.

"Yeah, great," he said, pushing aside the distasteful fare we had served him and smiling nostalgically as he thought back to noon.

"What did you have?"

"Three hot dogs, an ice cream cone, a couple of candy bars, and a Coke. Really filled me up," he said.

Lunch in the School Cafeteria is excellent for developing cavities and then, if there is a bit of horseplay, such as a game of catch with the mustard bottle,

for knocking out the teeth that would otherwise have to be filled.

Another interesting feature of high school is Study Hall, where students and faculty are brought together in the same room for regular periods. Anyone who has seen what goes on in Study Hall will appreciate the truth of the old saying, "You can lead a teen-ager to books, but you can't make him study." Or the other one, attributed to Benjamin Franklin, "A teen-ager and his books are soon parted." At the end of an hour of staring into space a few inches above an open volume, a teen-ager gathers up such necessary aids to concentration as a nail file, a bottle of nail polish, a package of Life Savers, a box of raisins, a pair of tweezers, and a mirror, and leaves the room mentally exhausted.

Assignments not completed in Study Hall can, of course, be finished at home. Working conditions are better here than in Study Hall, because the record player can be turned up loud enough to drown the sound of a pen scratching paper or the turning of pages. And the strain of intense cerebration can be relieved by stopping work, every few minutes, to watch television for half an hour.

There is also the availability of supplies, not so handy in Study Hall, without which my daughter would be unable to do any profound thinking:

> Peanut butter thickly spread
> On crispy crackers and on bread,
> Potato chips and chunks of cheese,
> Chocolates and cake—it's these
> With which my teen-age daughter crams
> For exams.

Some consider it dishonest for parents to help too much with their teen-ager's homework, and not really educational in the long run. Indeed, this is sometimes the line taken by parents themselves after the math assignments get too advanced for them. Or after the history paper which was ghosted, or guest-edited, comes back with a C— and the smart-aleck comment: "Unoriginal, superficial. Expression immature."

On the other hand, it is a splendid way for parents to learn something. I myself profited immensely from working on a paper on "Games and Pastimes in Puritan New England." And I learned a great deal from a paper for Senior English entitled "Chivalric Ideals in Sir Walter Scott's *Ivanhoe*," a paper that was causing me no end of trouble until I ran across a very helpful book from which it could be lifted almost verbatim. Why the paper, which was beautifully typed and enclosed in a cardboard cover on which I drew, with color crayons, a picture of a medieval knight on horseback, got a D, I shall never know. Some high school teachers simply lack critical judgment, while others read too much and recognize sources.

But however bitter your feelings about the ignorance and unfairness of your child's teacher, you should control the impulse to march right up to that feather-brained pedagogue and "tell him a few things," or go over his head to the Principal.

Once I went to my daughter's French teacher, thinking to ask nothing more than that the poor girl's grade be raised a couple of notches, and I have never been so humiliated in my life. Wishing to make a good impression, and emboldened by the fact that the young woman's name was Smith, I started right off speaking French to her, rattling off long, complicated sentences like *"Comment allez-vous?"* and *"Ouvrez la fenêtre."* Unhappily she took the linguistic ball away from me, speaking French so rapidly and with such an odd accent that I could catch only an occasional word. My daughter had failed to tell me that Mrs. Smith's maiden name was Jeanne-Françoise Noilly, and that she was born and educated in Paris and held the *Diplôme d'Études Supérieures* from the Sorbonne.

Then there was the time I called on the Principal merely to request that he make my son's English teacher cut down the reading assignments, which were getting too long for me. Here I was still in the middle of *Silas Marner,* a book with a very long middle, and the teacher had assigned *The Return of the Native* for next week, along with a written report on the characters, setting, and plot. What had brought me to the breaking point was that I misunderstood my son, thinking he said *Silas Lapham,* not *Silas Marner,* and was on the last chapter of *The Rise of Silas Lapham* before I discovered my error. This lost me at least three days and had me reading furiously to catch up.

The Principal listened sympathetically, when I told him politely but forcefully that the English teacher was sadistic and the assignments were altogether too long. I didn't mean to threaten him, but just for good measure I dropped the hint that one of my closest friends was a member of the School Board, which was partially true.

"I'll speak to Miss Wetherby," he reassured me.

"Thank you, sir," I said. "It's not just my son I'm thinking about, it's all the others." I, of course, was one of the others, but he could hardly have suspected.

He spoke to the English teacher, all right, and I have often wondered what he said. Anyhow, the assignments suddenly became twice as long, and the books twice as hard. From *The Return of the Native* we went to *War and Peace* and *The Decline and Fall of the Roman Empire,* which took Gibbon twenty-four years to write, and no wonder. Before, I had only stayed up a couple of hours later, to get the reading done, but now I also gave up watching *Gunsmoke* and the *Late Show.* I could have killed Miss Wetherby, and one of my pleasantest dreams—from which I awakened smiling—was doing so.

This is not to say that my teen-age son is not a reader, and a fast one, no matter how I myself plod along, framing the words on my lips. We spent a hundred dollars on a special after-hours course that did wonders for him:

> Our son has been given a speed-reading course,
>   Causing rate and retention to soar.
> Now he's able to read twice as fast twice as much
>   Of the trash he was reading before.

If you don't think my son is a reader, you ought to see the eagerness with which he grabs up the paper on Sunday morning, now that he has grown large enough to lift it all by himself. Often he snatches it out of sister's hands, or mine, in his impatience to

get the latest news of the world—the world, that is, of Li'l Abner and Dick Tracy. Or he goes directly for the classified ads, hoping someone is selling a second-hand carburetor that will function on his third-hand car. If he read the Great Books with the avidity he reads the comics and the classified ads, he would be another Clifton Fadiman or Mortimer Adler, with a bright future as a member of the advisory committee of the Book-of-the-Month Club.

I have said something about my abortive efforts to influence high school teachers. Parents can probably accomplish more if, instead of going it alone, they join a pressure group, such as the PTA. The only trouble about such a group is that the pressure, I have found, is on the members. I went to a meeting once, when I took part for three hours in a spirited discussion of a proposed change in the by-laws which would, if enacted, have raised the dues from two dollars a year to two dollars and twenty-five cents. The proposal was voted down by a narrow margin. I argued so persuasively against the increase in dues, hoping thereby to save twenty-five cents, that at the close of the meeting I was elected Treasurer, for a three-year term, and charged with finding ways of making up the rather alarming deficit.

It was this experience that led me to write these heartfelt lines:

> Get in and study, Junior, please,
>> Do all that you can do.
> Though I'm not fond of prodigies,
>> I cherish your IQ.
>
> Obey the teacher, break no rule,
>> And speed the blessed day
> When you will graduate from school
>> And I from PTA.

High School Commencement comes at last. It was worth all the effort, some parents are able to say with a straight face. The Valedictorian and Salutatorian (somebody else's children, and how such dull people could have such bright offspring you will never understand) make speeches, and so do the Principal and the Superintendent and the President of the Board of Education.

"As this graduating class goes forth to meet the challenge of life," says the Superintendent, "facing the future, burdening our shoulders—I mean shouldering our burdens. . . ." At this point he is handed a small piece of paper by the President of the Board of Education, assumed by the audience to be an important announcement he is supposed to make, perhaps that there is a fire in the dressing room directly behind the stage and no one should panic if he sees smoke and flames. Actually it says: "You had five minutes and you've gone fifteen. For God's sake, cut it off!"

Then the glee club sings (your child had a hacking cough the night of the tryouts), the orchestra plays (you were never very musical either), and the 368 graduates file across the stage, in alphabetical order.

The night my son graduated, only one student in that long line stumbled. Fortunately, he has quick reflexes, inherited from my wife's side of the family, and he almost saved himself by grabbing at the flag before he fell off the stage into the bass drum. It was a patriotic gesture that was wildly applauded.

After Commencement there is an all-night Beach Party which blows, in a few carefree hours, the forty-five hundred dollars accumulated by the Parents' Committee after years of cake baking and benefits and bazaars and white elephant sales. The party itself turns out to be a white elephant, the Name Band having gone to the wrong city and so having arrived only in time to play "Auld Lang Syne," one of the buses—the one containing the chaperones—breaking down on the way home, and the Senior Most Likely to Succeed, a nonswimmer, falling off the pier with his graduation suit on and having his title changed to the Senior Most Likely to Drown.

The next day your teen-ager, now a high-school graduate, embarks on a new phase in his career by sleeping twelve hours straight (and no telling how many hours crooked), getting up for dinner, and then going back to bed again.

You might try to get a nap yourself, if you can.

VI: Parties

When our children were small, a party might be messy but it was relatively inexpensive and not likely to provoke the neighbors into calling the police. Birthday parties were a success if there were a few simple games and plenty of ice cream, cake, and lemonade. At worst, some little fellow would throw up, after overindulging, and it would be a long time until the spot finally faded out of the living-room rug.

In those early years, however, we learned one simple technique about parties which proved invaluable when our children became teen-agers and we moved into big-league entertaining. The technique is to say to another parent, before this person with less experience or slower reflexes manages to blurt it out: "Let's have the party at *your* house. We'll furnish the dessert."

When two parents simultaneously make the same suggestion, there is likely to be an embarrassing pause. Someone's next line should then be, "Your house is so much nicer for entertaining." This may be hard to say, when you think the other house is a hovel, but with the issue a matter of such consequence, you should try to force out the words and even, if possible, look sincere.

Having the party at someone else's house is half the battle. At least it means that your house will not depreciate a couple of years in a single evening, undergoing the kind of aging that is sometimes seen, with a sense of shock, in a good friend after a severe illness. A house, however, doesn't recuperate after a party, unless it is nursed along by sundry painters, carpenters, glaziers, and rug menders—none of them paid for by Blue Cross.

I know of one house where, after a particularly vigorous party, they had to reset the foundation. It is true that, in this instance, teen-age guests were not wholly responsible, the structure having been weakened by termites. But, come to think of it, there probably are houses that have been weakened by teen-agers and finished off by termites. In either order, the combination is plenty destructive.

One of the best ways to keep from having a teenage party at your house, aside from not having teenagers, is not having a house. It may seem a lot of trouble to pitch a tent at the edge of town, and take it down every morning and hide it away, lest other parents get the idea that a tent party would be fun. Or to live in a trailer and be always on the move. But considering the alternative, no sacrifice is too great.

Another way to escape is to live in a house that is too small—maybe a tiny place over someone's garage. However, some parent is sure to say, after you have been first with the "Let's have it at *your* house" gambit, "But your house is so much cozier. And young people *like* to be crowded!"

Skillful as my wife and I are, we have sometimes

been boxed into having a party at our house. Either we were a little slow with our reactions or we tossed a coin for it, and it was *their* coin and the coin was obviously loaded.

I remember, for instance, the first time my daughter had a slumber party. We had never had a slumber party for our son, who is two years older, because boys just don't go in for such things, I hope. So it was a new and upsetting experience from which I have not yet fully recovered.

That night, six of my daughter's friends arrived, each with a sleeping bag, an overnight case, and her hair up in curlers.

"Going camping?" I asked cheerily when I let them in the front door.

They brushed past me without comment, probably thinking me the butler or, considering the hour, the night watchman, and trooped on upstairs to my daughter's room. After all, my question was pretty silly, when our guests were carrying no tents and only one of them had what looked like a portable stove. (As I found out later, it *was* a portable stove.)

The bathroom was in use for the next two hours, though I managed to slither in once, when they foolishly left the place unoccupied for a few seconds, to brush my teeth. No sooner had I got in, though, than someone was rattling the doorknob, so I just made a few passes at my molars and got out, trying to look nonchalant as I sauntered past the line of young women in my shorts. (Don't mistake me: I was in my shorts; they weren't.)

As I hightailed it to bed, I passed my daughter's room or, as she prefers to call it, pad. The door was slightly ajar, and I managed to get a quick look. It was the first time I had ever seen wall-to-wall sleeping bags. I would have seen a lot more, but someone slammed the door in my face, which, fortunately, I got out of the way of in time to receive nothing more than a slight bruise over the right cheekbone.

As the night wore on, it was clear that there were more sleeping bags than sleeping girls. Or sleeping anybody. It was a hard night.

The next morning I summed it up this way:

Last night my teen-age daughter had
A slumber party. May I add
I got no slumber, thanks to squealing,
Hi-fi, and such. And now I'm stealing
Away to work, warned by my mate:
"Be quiet, dear. They're sleeping late."

One thing I'll say for slumber parties—they're the cheapest kind. Other parties finally let you get to sleep, about two A.M., but they cost like the devil.

Take music. In our town we have what is known as the Dads' Band. This is a fine little group, playing piano, saxophone, bass fiddle, and banjo. The men in the band are all parents of teen-agers, and they are glad to play for nothing, or next to nothing. They specialize in the hit tunes of the Twenties and Thirties, the ones you can really dance to, like "The Sheik of Araby," "On the Sunny Side of the Street," and "Just a Gigolo," and every now and then there is a waltz, slow and dreamy.

"Remember that one?" my wife is likely to ask me, her eyes fogging over.

"Sure do," I say. "The big hit of 1933. Brings back all sorts of memories—the banks closed, 3.2 beer...." I may become so emboldened as to say, "Let's try this one. I think it's slow enough."

But the teen-agers absolutely refuse to have the Dads' Band any more.

"Oh, I know they're all friends of yours," my daughter said once, when she was planning a dance and I suggested—little old economical me—that the Dads' Band would be just the ticket. "But they play those awful oldies and they're just amateurs. Unless we can have something better, we'll give up the dance and go bowling. Why can't we have a name band?"

"Well, they have a name, haven't they? They're the Dads' Band," I said.

"Oh, come off it," she said. "I mean somebody who really is somebody and has made records and been on TV and everything."

"Like Lawrence Welk?" I asked sarcastically. "With Perry Como for a soloist?"

"Yes," she said in all seriousness, "or Glenn Miller or Guy Lombardo."

I didn't bother to ask her if she had any idea what that would cost, or whether she would like to have Judy Garland and Bing Crosby thrown in to sing along with Perry. She had enough big ideas without my giving her any more.

Another thing about the music at teen-age parties, which makes me, frankly, a little envious of persons who are hard of hearing:

> There's this about
> The teen-age crowd:
> They like their music
> Good and loud.
>
> And I'm not hep,
> I lack the knack.
> It sends me, but
> I don't come back.

Of course I know the music has to be loud. Otherwise you might be able to hear what the other person was saying and be tempted to strike up an intelligent conversation, which would be out of place.

Let's go on to refreshments. Only "refreshments" is the wrong word for what you have to serve at a teen-age party these days. "Buffet supper" is more like it, and your one chance of getting by without champagne and caviar is to cite the state liquor law and to explain that the only good caviar comes from Russia, and you refuse to have any truck with those Communist fish.

But there is no excuse for not having prime ribs and cold roast turkey and everything pertaining thereto, such as a couple of men in white jackets and tall chefs' hats (tall hats for short chefs) to do the carving. And be sure they are professionals, or at least strangers—there's no use trying to put Uncle Ned and Cousin George into white jackets. The kids just won't accept substitutes.

And a man in a red jacket, looking as if he has just come in from a fox hunt, to ladle out the punch.

And a couple of girls with white uniforms and French accents, to pour the coffee and bring in the dessert and clear off the tables. (Here, with a bow to automation, I must admit that nowadays you can get by with a Coke machine, which, though fairly expensive to install, gives you a percentage of the take.)

And a man with a flashlight to park cars, and to flash his flashlight into parked cars.

Such parties, I probably need not reiterate, are expensive. In time, though, with the government helping everyone else, it may be possible to apply for federal aid. Or, if the party was held at your house, you may be able to have the place declared a disaster area, and get a low-interest loan until you are on your feet again.

One thing that costs no money at a teen-age party is chaperones. In general there are two types:

1. Those who take the assignment seriously and act like house detectives or members of the FBI, beating the bushes (literally) for couples who need to be uncoupled, and peering suspiciously under tables. They may overlook cheek-to-cheek dancing but not mouth-to-mouth, even though purportedly for purposes of resuscitation.

2. Those who see no evil, speak only when spoken to, and are hard to find in case of an emergency. What kind of an emergency? Well, a bunch of party-crashing boys who ought to be thrown out but are not because they are bigger and more numerous than the boys at the party. Or a boy and girl who are suddenly discovered to be missing and everybody looks all over for them and the tension mounts almost to hysteria until someone remembers that they never came. Or a greedy youth who gets his hand caught in the Coke machine, and it serves him right, trying to extract two bottles at once and save a dime. Or a girl who had something to drink that wasn't officially served at the party and she passes out cold and somebody has to phone her parents and tell them to come and get her because she is—uh—sick.

Of the two types, the detectives and the defectives, the first is a great favorite of parents, except the parents of youngsters who get into trouble because of

the nosiness and prejudice of the chaperone. The second is a great favorite of teen-agers, without exception.

The canny host has one of the first type and one of the second. The two tend to cancel each other out, which is just like having no chaperone at all, but looks better.

The word "chaperone," I recently discovered, comes from the French *chape,* "a hood."

Whoever dreamed up the word was probably confused, or had never been a chaperone. There are usually a few hoods at a teen-age dance, but they are not chaperones.

To sum up:

> Chaperoning a party?
> I'm sorry it's true,
> But here, very briefly,
> Is what you must do:
>
> Provide transportation,
> No matter from where,
> And lend your best records
> And seem not to care,
>
> Help hang decorations,
> Assist with the cooking,
> And keep your eyes open
> Without ever looking.

VII: Cars

I find it hard to imagine what it was like before the automobile. Did the children fight over who could have the family horse and buggy? Were mother and father left at home, peering at a stereopticon view of the Grand Canyon for the hundredth time, while Junior harnessed up the mare and went trotting off to a husking bee or a square dance?

Did the children insist on having a horse and buggy of their own? And did they no sooner get what they wanted than they started taking it apart—removing the mudguards, fastening a chrome disk over the wooden spokes, putting smaller wheels in the front, and making such alterations in the horse as were not fatal?

I have a feeling that pre-automobile parents had an easier time of it than we do today. A father, who in those days knew as much as anyone in the family about the care and feeding of a horse, was not put in the humiliating position of standing by helplessly while his son traced the motor failure to a loose wire in the distributor. Parents had less concern for the safety of their teen-agers in a one-horsepower vehicle on a country lane than in a three-hundred-horse-power vehicle on a crowded freeway. And who will deny that drunken drivers are more dangerous—and more numerous—than drunken horses?

But there is no use looking back, wistfully. The automobile is here to stay, at least until it is super-seded by the family rocket ship, in which teen-agers will park on the dark side of the moon:

> When skies are full of small jet planes
> That clutter up the airy lanes,
> When lady pilots zoom around
> At speeds exceeding that of sound,
> When Junior, still a trifle wet
> Behind the ears, takes out the jet
> And strips it down to very socket
> To race a space ship or a rocket,
> When airway cops, with sirens loud,
> Come darting from behind a cloud,

When conversation can't be heard
And scenery is faint and blurred,
When shopping place or picnic spot
A hundred miles is overshot,
And airports landed after dark on
Have not a single place to park on—
When this occurs, some distant year,
I'll not regret that I'm not here.

I remember with what pride and relief I received
the news that my son had passed the driving test and
obtained his license. No longer would I have to drive
him on a date, sitting behind the wheel like a chauf-
feur, when I took him and some giggly girl to a
movie.

"What time will the second feature be over?" I
asked the girl in the ticket booth.

"Exactly 11:22," she said.

Then, after I synchronized my watch with the clock on the wall behind her, I drove home and spent the evening until I had to drive back to the theater and pick up my passengers. I preferred this to parking in front of the theater with all the other fathers, each of us like a cab driver waiting for a fare. Usually, during the four hours or so I had at home, I watched television, but sometimes I went to bed, setting the alarm clock for, say, 11:10. From much practice, I got so I could cut it pretty fine, setting the alarm for as late as 11:16. This meant leaping out of bed while still not quite awake, running through the house, jumping into the car, driving at precisely the maximum speed limit, and arriving in front of the movie theater just as my son and his girl friend emerged, smelling of popcorn. Despite the gasoline that would be consumed in four hours, I was often tempted to leave the engine running—to get another thirty seconds of shut-eye.

No longer either, now that my son had his driver's license, would I suffer the embarrassment I endured after he got his learner's permit. Then, though he could drive, I had to go along, sitting next to him, where I could grab the wheel or slam my foot on the brake. Nights when he drove up to the top of Mount Lookout with his girl for an hour of smooching, I got into the back seat, after we parked, and read a magazine by flashlight or walked down the road a piece. There were nights when I thought I would freeze to death.

And then there were those double dates, when neither boy had more than a learner's permit (to drive, that is), and I sat in one corner of the back seat all evening and tried to be inconspicuous or, ideally, invisible.

Now, though, he could drive the car all by himself, and pick up the cleaning and get the groceries and do a dozen other useful chores. My wife and I blessed the Department of Motor Vehicles that issued him his license, and we thought of all the things we could do in the time saved from running a taxi service or co-piloting.

But our rejoicing was cut short when we learned that the cost of accident and public liability insurance on our car nearly doubled the moment we mentioned to our agent, whom we had considered a friend, that the car was now and then driven by a male under twenty-five years of age.

And though he said, "Yeah, sure," when we told our son to pick up the cleaning or get the groceries, he seldom remembered to do so, with more important things—such as basketball and girls—on his mind. So we got the groceries and the cleaning ourselves, as before, only now our son was away somewhere with the car and we had to walk. Fortunately, we live close in, and the grocery store and the cleaner

are only a half mile and a mile away, respectively—
in opposite directions.

Two years after our son obtained his driver's
license, our daughter got hers. As for me, I bought a
bicycle. My wife, who has trouble with her arches,
bought some British walkers.

Then a series of events led me to think that the
transportation situation in our household needed re-
vamping.

First, my bicycle was stolen.

Second, my wife's chiropodist raised his fee from
$5.00 to $8.00 a visit, and the visits were getting
more frequent. (I hate to confess this, but I began to
think my wife had fallen in love with her chiropodist, she went to him so often, and I sat at home imagining all sorts of things about his fondling her
feet.)

Third, one day I needed to know the make of our
car, while filling out a questionnaire, and I couldn't
remember.

Decisions have always been hard for me, and I
couldn't bear to go on, day after day, deciding who—
my son or my daughter—would get the car. Usually
I said, "Well, ask your mother." But this was weak of
me, and I hated myself for it.

So we bought a second car.

"What kind shall we get?" I asked one night at
dinner. This was a mistake. I should have asked no

one, but simply gone out and bought something cheap and simple and conservative and with a good trade-in value.

"I know," my son said. "I know just the car."

And that is how we came to buy something expensive and complicated and flashy and hard to trade in. It was a foreign car, with a right-hand drive that was intended, apparently, for left-handed people. It was also a convertible, with a canvas top that went up hard but came down easily, especially in a high wind. One windy day it blew off completely and we could never get it back on and the car ceased to be a convertible. The first time we had to have something repaired, which was after we had driven about two hundred miles, we discovered that certain spare parts, such as the one we needed, had to be ordered from the factory, in Trieste.

I know about the poor trade-in value, because we kept the car only three months, and got about half what we paid for it. We would have got rid of it sooner, but there was no use trying to sell it when it wouldn't run, and we were waiting for that spare part.

"I still think it's a good car," my son said. "We just happened to get a lemon."

He must have been right, because it left a sour taste in my mouth for a long time.

The second second car was a great success, popular with everyone. It was not only expensive but, I am glad to say, looked it. My wife liked it because of the gold threads in the imported upholstery—imported, I think, from Fort Knox. My daughter liked it because of the radio, which would run even when the ignition was not on and was unusually loud. My son liked it because of the way it would "corner," that is, go around a sharp corner at high speed without turning over—in fact doing nothing more than frightening the occupants and burning the tread off the tires.

"The torque is great, Dad," my son said as we sat in this new car in front of the house.

"I'm glad to hear it," I said, not having the slightest idea of what torque is but not wishing to appear any more ignorant than necessary.

"Both the pull-in torque and the pull-out torque," he added, obviously well-satisfied.

"Splendid," I said, happy to learn that torque comes in two varieties and we had both of them, apparently as standard equipment.

"Keep your eyes on the tachometer," he said, "while I rev her up."

"It doesn't seem to be doing anything," I said, after he had raced the motor for several seconds.

"Sure it is," he said. "Boy, look at those rpm's!" Then, noticing that I was peering intently at a little dial on which the hand had not moved a particle, "That's not the tachometer, Dad, that's the altimeter." He turned off the motor and sat for a moment with a look of disgust on his face. Then he got out, slamming the door harder than necessary.

I have told why my wife and daughter and son liked the new second car. I, too, liked it, and had my own reason. I liked it because, unlike the foreign car it replaced, it ran most of the time.

And when I say it ran most of the time, I mean it. Somebody was always driving this new second car. Nobody wanted to drive the old family car any more, so my wife and I could have it—except for those times, which became more and more frequent, when my son had to have a car and my daughter had to have a car and my wife and I had to have a car.

So we bought a third car.

This third car was secondhand. We cut out the dealer and bought it from a friend, which meant that we paid more than it was worth, not wishing to haggle over a few hundred dollars. It was a 1952 model, that year, according to the teen-age set, having been a good year for this make of car. Teen-agers know cars the way some people know wines, and this was apparently a vintage year. We could have bought a 1954 model, in obviously better condition, for less, but my son had to have a 1952, this being the last year they had that particular insignia on the radiator and a light inside the glove compartment. Besides, this ten-year-old car had only 24,000 miles on it, and since we were dealing with a friend we could hardly ask whether the speedometer had been turned back.

At any rate, we made this third car our son's **very own**. After all, he put ten dollars of his own **money** into it. My wife and I were not sure we had done the right thing:

Our teen-age son has recently won
  A battle he's waged for years.
Now he owns a car and, frankly, we are
  Full of terrible, gnawing fears.

Will he drive too fast? Will he try to go past
  On a road that is narrow and winding?
Will he fail to stop when he's hailed by a cop,
  Despite all our constant reminding?

Will he race a train? Will a trace remain
   Of our son if it ends in a tie?
What will happen if he should park on a cliff
   And leave the car running in high?

So his mother is blue, and I am too,
   As we dream of catastrophe.
And we worry and fret and somehow forget
   How much better he drives than we.

Shortly afterward, not wishing to show favoritism, we let our daughter have a car of her own. To do this, we traded in our new second car, which was barely broken in, for a car that was better for my daughter. That is, it has a mirror in the dashboard that is a great convenience when she needs to apply lipstick, and the hub caps are simply darling. Because the car we traded in was larger and more expensive and less than a year old, we managed to get this small new car for our daughter for only twelve hundred dollars extra.

The chief problem now is the garage. What do you do when you have three cars and a two-car garage? Worse than that, when half the garage is filled with garden tools and trash barrels and excess furniture and suitcases, as well as old clothes and bundles of newspapers that the Salvation Army would have collected if we had remembered to tell them what day we would be home. This accumulation of impedimenta reduces our two-car garage to what is, in effect, a one-car garage.

The simple solution would seem to be to put the newest car, my daughter's, inside, it being the one most worth protecting. But one of the others, the family car, has a leak around the windows that lets the rain in. So why not put my daughter's car inside in good weather and the family car when it rains?

I'll tell you why. My son's car is in there all the time, dismantled and impossible to move, with parts lying all around:

> He's working on his car. That is,
>   With zeal and no restraint
> He's taken off the grille in front,
>   The bumper guards, the paint.
>
> He's taken off the maker's mark
>   Wherever it appeared,
> He's taken off the fenders, though
>   We almost interfered.
>
> He's taken off the hub caps and
>   The chrome along the side,
> The handles from the doors, as well. . . .
>   Yes, he has scraped and pried
>
> And worked with hammers, pliers, wrench,
>   And fingers strong and deft
> Until what he has taken off
>   Is more than what is left.

What I foresee is a second garage. Or, since there isn't room on our lot for another garage, another house.

At last we have enough cars that we no longer need to figure out ways of getting a ride with friends, or having them pick up our children to take them to Pilgrim Fellowship or to dancing class. Now they are doing this to us, and I am getting mighty tired of it.

But if the gas and oil and tires and repairs and insurance and licenses and depreciation total several thousand dollars a year, there is a bright side to it all. As my wife said one day at the service station, while we were watching the little meter whiz around, "Don't forget. They give Green Stamps."

There are those who feel sorry for me, when they see me pumping uphill on my bicycle, with a wire basket loaded with groceries, while my wife and son and daughter are off somewhere with the three cars. But I have read several authoritative articles on the importance of regular exercise to middle-aged men, and how good cycling is for the heart. The members of my family, always unselfish and considerate, have done me a great service. I may live ten years longer, as a result, and go on earning the money for which they have so many uses.

I have also read several articles, which I recommend to fellow fathers, about how bad it is for the heart to give way to a fit of anger, kicking the door of an empty garage.

What should you do when you feel your self-control slipping? Just hop onto your bicycle and pedal off, very fast.

VIII: Conversation

Conversation with a teen-ager is almost impossible, I have discovered, unless by chance you also are a teen-ager. In that case it is ridiculously easy or, when overheard by an adult, easily ridiculous.

It does no good for an adult to pretend to be a teen-ager for the sake of sliding into a conversation. Teen-agers have ways of detecting that you are an adult, even if you have a flattop haircut and wear a shirt with an unfunctional button on the back of the collar. I know a man who had removable braces that he could pop into his mouth, and a make-up pencil for stippling his face with realistic pimples, but they saw through his disguise.

The worst thing you can do in an effort to ingratiate yourself is to use teen-age slang. That gives you away at once, because the expression you picked up a month ago is probably now out of date, or means just the opposite of what it did then.

Take the word "tough." I had gone along for years thinking the word meant difficult, as in a "tough assignment," or unfortunate, as in a "tough break," or sturdy, as in a "tough physique," or hardened in vice, as in a "tough customer." My mental image of a "tough" was a slouching fellow in a turtleneck sweater, with a cigarette hanging out of the corner of his mouth and a blackjack or a switchblade knife in his pocket. I have always been afraid of toughs and have tried to keep out of their way, because I myself am what might be called, if anyone had thought of it (and I am glad no one has), a "tender."

With this concept of "tough" in mind, I was startled, a couple of years ago, when my daughter used the word in connection with a friend of hers whom I had thought a sweet, well-mannered girl.

"Linda is tough," I clearly heard her say, or as clearly as I hear anything she says.

"Surely you don't mean Linda Waterman," I said.

"Yes, I do," my daughter said firmly. "She's the toughest girl in my class, and maybe in the whole school."

I was shocked. Apparently I was no judge of character, especially in teen-agers. I wondered whether

Linda was pulling the wool over the eyes of other adults also. Or was I, a poor judge of character, the only one who was taken in?

"Do her parents know?" I asked.

"Know what?"

"Do they know she has the reputation around school of being tough?"

"I don't dig you," my daughter said in a tone that was a blend of incredulity and disgust.

"I just can't believe Linda is tough," I said.

"Well, she is," my daughter maintained stoutly. "She's smart and good-looking and has a keen personality and has lots of clothes and goes with the neatest boy in the class and drives a Porsche. So if she isn't tough, I don't know who is."

About this time I woke up to the semantic change that had taken place in the word "tough" in teen-age usage, though not as yet recorded in the dictionary. Linda wasn't a tough, or at least not my kind of tough. My daughter had not demeaned her but had bestowed upon her the highest accolade, for to be tough, in her set, was to be what in my boyhood was the ultimate in all that is admirable and enviable. "Tough" must be derived from "tough competition," though I am only guessing.

"I see," I said, visibly relieved to learn that I had not misjudged Linda, after all. "She's the cat's whiskers."

"Just what do you mean by that?" my daughter

asked, thinking I was maligning her friend, perhaps suggesting that she needed a depilatory.

"The cat's whiskers is about the same as the cat's meow," I explained, "and when I was young we applied it to a girl who was a lollapalooza."

"You and your crazy words," my daughter said. "Well, I can't stick around gassing any longer. Jeanne wants me to come over to her pad and spin a few platters. Beseenya."

I went through much the same sequence of puzzlement and enlightenment when I discovered that a square is no longer a parallelogram having four equal sides and four right angles, but a person rejected by the gang. To teen-agers, almost all adults are squares. That is to say, they are misfits, square pegs in the round holes of society, creatures to be ridiculed, pitied, or—the best solution, if it can be arranged—avoided.

Of course if you talk to teen-agers as if you are an adult talking to adults, for a few wonderful minutes they will be flattered to death, and you may be able to convey an idea or two. You will have to work fast, however, before their eyes begin to get that glassy, uninterested look or they turn up the record player to drown you out. By such signs you will know that they have made the transition from being flattered to death to being bored to death.

But you should never be long-winded, anyhow. You may be wanting to kill time, but teen-agers have

to make every minute count. They have important things to do, such as going to a drive-in for a hamburger right after dinner, or seeing a movie they have seen only once before. You can't expect them to stand around listening to you shoot the breeze, unless you are a basketball hero or someone who really has something to say, such as a TV comic.

While I am at it, let me suggest that you not talk down to teen-agers. This may seem unnecessary advice, since the teen-ager is probably six or eight inches taller than you are, and you have to keep jumping up, as if you were shooting a basket, to get within speaking distance of his ear. It's even worse if you remain sitting while the teen-ager politely stands by your chair, shuffling uneasily.

And another thing. Speak distinctly. Don't think you can mumble the way *they* do when they speak to each other. They are not really mumbling; they are speaking Teenese, a dialect akin to Cantonese.

"Putona nother thasstoo sloforme," one of them says to another.

"Herza beatchul gofor," the other responds.[1]

By the way, when you speak to teen-agers, don't mistake attention for interest. A clever young person can listen to you with spellbound look for all of ten minutes, while you hold forth on the world situation or your vacation trip to Maine. Yet that flighty little

[1] Or, in Adult English: "Put on another. That's too slow for me." And the response: "Here's a beat you'll go for."

mind is miles away, at a bowling alley or in a parked car.

I had an experience with a teen-age friend of my son's that cooled me off considerably.

"I have had quite a bit of military service," I said, with my customary modesty.

"Oh, you have?" he said.

He should never have asked this searching question, betraying his intense interest in national defense and the not inconsiderable part I played therein.

"Yes, I served in the antiaircraft artillery in two wars," I said. Then I added, because I saw his gaze turning to my shelf of Civil War books, "World War II and the Korean War."

"Hunh," he said, obviously wishing to hear more.

Since I had not had an interested audience for some time, I went into all the details, making my exploits as spine-tingling as possible, considering that in neither war had I been closer to enemy action than Washington, D.C., where I sustained a bad bruise when I caught my hand in a mimeograph machine.

"Just a minute," I said, at the height of my narrative. "I want to show you some souvenirs of the fighting in New Guinea. I'll get them from my room." They were genuine articles, all right—Japanese rifles and bayonets and grenades—and if I did not explain that they were brought back to me by a cousin who had been out there in the Quarter-master Corps, it was because I had to omit a few nonessentials for the sake of dramatic unity. I left him on the edge of his chair.

When I got back with my armload of Japanese weapons, he was gone, and I saw a car pulling out of our driveway at high speed. He had, as I said, been on the edge of his chair, and he may also have been wearing track shoes.

Ever since, I have confined the tale of my military activities to adult audiences, mostly people who came to our house for dinner and were too polite to leave right after eating.

My mention of dinner reminds me that my wife has always cherished the hope that we would get around to some uplifting, or at least educational, conversation at the dinner table with our children.

"We shouldn't just sit there and munch and gulp," she said. "We should talk about things."

"Like what?" I asked.

"Current events and philosophical problems and literature," she said. "The children might learn something. It would stimulate their thinking." Then, as a practical afterthought, "And they might not eat so fast."

As I recall, we tried it three times. The first time, I brought a volume of Plato to the table and after I had eaten a few bites started reading one of the Dialogues, thinking to stir up a discussion on the

concept of virtue. I hadn't read it for some time (twenty-five years, to be exact), and I had forgotten how hard it was to understand. It was with some relief to me that my son had to leave to go to a basketball game and my daughter was called to the phone —and never came back—before I finished the Dialogue and was ready for discussion. I resolved to bone up before my next presentation. For some reason, we never got around to Plato again.

The second time, I launched into a discussion of the drain on our gold reserves and the stability of our currency and the functioning of the World Bank. This time I had prepared thoroughly, having read one entire article in *The Reader's Digest,* which I had underlined and brought to the table. I held forth eloquently, was really quite pleased with my-

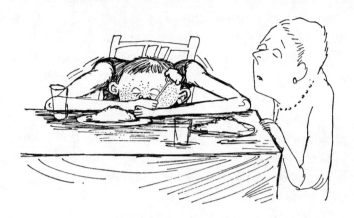

self, and didn't mind too much that my food was stone cold when I finally got around to eating it.

"What do *you* think?" I asked my son, wishing to draw him into the discussion. "Do you think we're facing an era of inflation?"

"Inflation's already here, Dad," he said. "That's why I've been telling you I need five bucks a week more on my allowance."

The discussion, I could see, was taking an unwholesome turn, and I excused myself from the table, feeling a sharp pain in the region of my wallet.

The third time, my wife made a valiant try. She had prepared an excellent quiz on current events in Africa, and passed around the questions just after she passed around the gravy. It was a good idea, except that my daughter, reaching for a sheet of questions, struck the edge of the gravy bowl, and by the time we had finished mopping up the table and trying to get the spot out of the rug, and my daughter had changed her dress, no one was in any mood for questions on Mboya, Uganda, Lumumba, Bandundo, and Bwanamkubwa.

It was our last attempt at intellectual conversation at the dinner table. Now we just eat, the silence broken only when someone chews a piece of celery or has a coughing fit or mumbles, "Pass me the salt." You shouldn't talk with your mouth full, anyhow.

This is not to say that there is no conversation in homes where there are teen-agers. But it is likely to be a conversation of which you hear only one end. I refer, of course, to what goes on around and through the telephone.

With us, our daughter is the one who is on the phone the most. Or perhaps I should put it another way:

I said, "My daughter's on the phone,"
But I was wrong. I should have known,
Considering the way she falls
From chair to floor, and twists and sprawls
And lies there, phoning, on her back
For hours of unimportant yak,
She isn't on the phone—no, sir—
The phone's on her.

When you are trying to telephone home during the hours your teen-ager is there, and you get the busy signal, you can be sure of one thing: the line will stay busy for a long time. You can, of course, interrupt whatever essential work you are engaged in and try again every two or three minutes, on the chance that you will hit the split-second period after one conversation ends and before the next begins. This is possible, but the law of averages is against you.

So you can telephone a neighbor and ask her to relay your message.

Or you can send a telegram.

Or you can write your message on a small piece of paper, insert it in a capsule, and dispatch it by carrier pigeon.

Or you can say to hell with it and change your plans, whatever they were.

Or, if freedom of communication means more to you than money, you can put in a separate line for your teen-ager and have your own phone, under lock and key, and an unlisted number.

It does no good to get mad, and it also does no good for me to tell you this. I get mad myself, just thinking about it.

One thing about telephone calls when you are at home. If the phone rings and you answer it, it's not for you. If the phone rings and you don't answer it, it is. There is something awfully spooky about this.

Come to think of it, you may derive a certain satisfaction, or catharsis, out of getting mad. Yanking out the telephone wires and stamping on the telephone until it is a mass of switches, gears, and bits of plastic is one way of getting relief, if you really want to let yourself go. But this is expensive, as you will discover when the repairman comes. And he may say something that will make you angry all over again—such as "Naughty, naughty!"

My own way to let off steam is to stick pins into a small, bearded figure I have carved out of a cake of soap. It isn't much of a likeness, because I'm not much of a sculptor, but it's supposed to be Alexander Graham Bell.

IX: Hair and teeth

As my own hair grows sparser, I am increasingly envious of teen-age youths who have such an abundance. Often I find myself coveting the hair of some callow lad whose hairline starts only an inch or so above his eyebrows and sweeps down over the back of his collar. If only, I find myself musing, a surgeon could remove a few patches of this luxuriant growth, follicles and all, and replant it on my head like a piece of sod. The youngster wouldn't miss it—in fact it would make him appear a little less Neanderthal —and I would be helped mightily. You can get a blood transfusion. Why not a hair transfusion?

I can imagine myself going not to a barber but to a doctor, a hirsutologist.

Instead of saying, "Shall I take a little off the top" he would say, holding a scalpel in one hand and a thick mat of hair, from a hair bank, in the other, "Shall I put a little on the top?"

"Yes," I would say, peering at myself in the mirror and pointing to the place in the crown of my head where I look like a freshly shorn monk, "and about a two-inch strip along the top of my forehead, if you don't mind."

Matching my envy is my fascination with what teen-agers do with what they have. Were they to put half as much inventiveness and painstaking effort into other activities, they would not only make important breakthroughs in science but achieve the three-minute mile and the eighteen-foot pole vault.

As I see it, with the jaundiced eye of one whose scalp is showing:

Teen-age boys have zany haircuts,
Absurd, exotic, really rare cuts:
The duck tail, and the suavely sheikish,
The cheek-long sideburns, slightly freakish,
The butch, the flattop, and the crew cut,
Whatever is the fad, the new cut.
Although *inside* the teen-age skull
There oftentimes may be a lull,
To compensate for such passivity
Outside the skull there's great activity.

My wife believes there would be an end to juvenile delinquency if teen-age bads (a word I recently picked up from my son) were required to keep their hair short. Her theory is that dandified (at first I thought the word was dandruffied) long hair leads to a kind of bravado that, in turn, leads to reckless driving, petty thievery, and glue-sniffing. So she proposes a ten-dollar fine for any teen-ager who lets his hair grow longer than half an inch. To enforce the law, she would have policemen equipped with night sticks calibrated, for measuring, along the side.

My own suggestion is to let teen-agers wear their hair as long as they wish, but prohibit their carrying pocket combs. This would soon reduce their hair to such a hopeless tangle that they would beg for a crew cut.

If my wife has been unable to put her theory into general practice, she has at least done something about it in our own home. Two unhappy developments, occurring at approximately the same time, stung her into action: (1) our son took to wearing his hair so long that we expected him any day to appear in a leather jacket with the insignia of a teen-age gang specializing in mugging, and (2) haircuts went up to two dollars.

Actually, what she took into her own hands was a pair of Handy Home Hair Klippers, purchased on sale for $6.98. She talked over her plans with me.

"I'll practice on you first," she said. "Your hair is easy."

"No thanks," I protested. I had visions of tonsorial mayhem, forcing me to keep my hat on indoors and pretending I was a detective or a newspaper reporter like Walter Winchell.

"Come on," she said in a tone half coaxing and half (or two-thirds) threatening. "All you need is a little off around the edges, and that isn't worth any two dollars. Besides, think of the time you'll save, not having to wait your turn in the barber shop."

"But I don't mind waiting," I said. "I relax, and I visit with people." And where else was I going to read *Playboy* and *Adam*? "Try it on Happy first," I said. Happy is our dog and has a lot more hair than I have.

"Don't be a coward," she said. "I'll be very careful."

In the end she had her way, as always. She sat me on a stool in the kitchen, with a towel around my neck, plugged in the clippers, and went to work. When she was through, I hurried to a mirror, expecting to look like Yul Brynner but less evenly.

However, it wasn't a bad job at all. A little high in back, perhaps, and a gouged spot over my left ear, but not so bad. In a month or so—after about three more tries on me—my wife was ready to tackle our son.

The first time she broached the subject, thoughtlessly holding the clippers in her hand, he took one quick look at the instrument and ran from the house.

In fact he stayed overnight with a friend, and I feared was gone for good.

"Next time," I told my wife, "be more subtle. Don't brandish those clippers under his nose."

He came back, all right, though for a while he held one hand on his head, shielding his hair, even at the dinner table.

My wife is a stubborn woman, and the longer our teen-age son's hair grew, the more determined she was to cut it short. What finally got him into the barber's chair in the kitchen, with a towel around his neck, I don't know. It may have been the five dollars my wife offered him. It may have been her promise to take off only a teeny-weeny little bit, a promise she wrote in red ink, to make it look like blood. It may have been that we were going on a month's camping trip into the Canadian Rockies, where he would see very few people and where it would not be thought peculiar to wear a stocking cap night and day.

I'll never forget that first homemade haircut. Expecting trouble, I had thoughtfully given the boy a tranquilizer, telling him it was a vitamin pill. Even then, it was a traumatic experience. You would have thought my wife, with those electric clippers in her hand, was a dentist with a drill, or a doctor about to perform an appendectomy without an anesthetic.

"Look out!" my son screamed, while the clippers

were still six inches from his hair. "You're getting it too short."

"Take it easy," I said, tightening my half nelson and sidestepping the kick that would otherwise have caught me just below the knee. "She hasn't even started yet."

"I want to watch in the mirror," my son said in the tone of a condemned man making a last request.

So I got him a hand mirror, into which he peered suspiciously. And, on his further demand, I held a second mirror behind him so that he could see what was going on in crucial areas of the neck and back of the head. From time to time he cringed, ducked, or uttered the heart-rending cries of a victim of forcible rape.

When it was all over, our son was not so much deflowered as deforested. The floor was covered with hair, seemingly enough to stuff a mattress. My wife collapsed on the kitchen stool, still holding the electric clippers, which continued to whir away until she remembered to turn them off. It was nothing more than a case of nervous exhaustion, and after a few hours she was able to walk around without help and keep down broth and crackers. I myself suffered only a temporary numbness in my right arm from holding the rearview mirror in place during the lengthy operation. Brisk rubbing restored circulation.

Our son, though, was hard hit. The way he raced

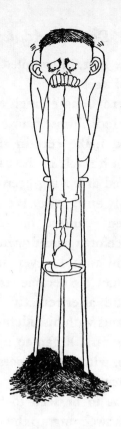

to the bathroom, I thought he was going to throw up, and I followed as far as the bathroom door, hoping to be of any possible assistance, such as holding his head. But he simply wished to look at himself in the medicine chest mirror, under a strong light.

"I'm ruined," he moaned, after gazing intently at his reflection, "absolutely ruined." He sounded for all the world like a man in a Victorian novel who had just lost his life's savings.

"It's only a little hair," I consoled him. "It'll grow back in a couple of weeks."

He left the mirror long enough to slam the door in my face and lock himself into the bathroom. After listening to make certain that he was not planning to drown himself in the bathtub, I tiptoed away, heavy-hearted at having been *particeps crimi-nis* in the dastardly enterprise. We might well have inflicted permanent damage on the lad's psyche, making him henceforth withdrawn and antisocial.

Though my son would never again permit his mother to cut his hair, he became fascinated with the electric clippers and, after tentative and exceedingly cautious experiments with his sideburns and the area directly above his ears, began to cut his own hair. How he does this, with the clippers in one hand, a mirror in the other, and two other mirrors wedged into his collar, has to be seen to be believed. My only part in this is sweeping up the hair and putting away the clippers, mirrors, scissors, comb, tweezers, and other items which our do-it-yourself barber leaves strewn about, his mother refusing to be of the slightest assistance now that her tonsorial skill has been questioned.

Oh yes, I also pay my son a dollar and seventy-five cents—saving a quarter on what he would otherwise spend at the barbershop—every time he cuts his hair. After a couple of weeks during which I almost went bankrupt, we came to a belated understanding about this: he could cut his hair every day, if he wished, but I would pay him for only one haircut a week.

My son has a pretty good business head, on which, I am happy to say, the hair is now kept to a reasonable length, and his mother no longer needs to worry about his being on the downhill road to delinquency. As for me, since she keeps my thinning hair cut close to the skull, she has no worry about my going astray. If I did, I would soon be rounded up, easily identified as an escaped convict.

But enough about my son's hair. Let me tell you about my daughter's teeth, another story with tragic aspects and economic overtones.

When my daughter was about thirteen, she had to have her teeth straightened. This was not made necessary, I hasten to say, by anything we had done to her. My wife and I have been tempted, but we are people of remarkable self-restraint.

No, her teeth just grew that way. And as soon as she learned a little about heredity and genes and that sort of thing, she was pretty resentful toward us. Not that they were really so bad—the front uppers simply looked like a small cowcatcher or, when operating on corn on the cob, like a bulldozer. In my own youth, before the development of orthodontia, they would have been left as they were, and no one would have given them a thought, except maybe an occa-

sional sentimentalist, who would have murmured,
"poor child," or some coward who was fearful of
being bitten.

I thought a little matter of teeth-straightening
wouldn't amount to much. But that was before I
went to the dentist, who after a professional inspec-
tion of my daughter's teeth and a few thoughts about
the new home he was building looked me straight
in the eye and said his bill would be nine hundred
dollars. Of course I could pay on the easy, lay-away
plan—five dollars a month, sixty dollars a year—
and in the brief span of fifteen years I wouldn't owe
him a penny.

Subsequently I met a woman who was having
much the same work done on her daughter, and she
said she was paying a thousand dollars. At first I
congratulated myself on having saved a hundred

dollars, but later I began to worry that I was getting too *cheap* a job, and after a while—*boing!* they would spring back into their old rabbity position.

The whole dismal experience led me to write a poem which, I am happy to say, I sold to a magazine for enough to cover my obligation to the dentist until I could take on a second job. These sad but lucrative lines were:

> My daughter has an orthodontist
> Around whom I appear my gauntest
> And wear my suit that's worn and seedy,
> In hope he'll class me with the needy.
>
> Yet months from now, I have no doubt,
> When bands are off and she goes out
> With straightened teeth and gleaming glances,
> I'll be in straitened circumstances.

By moonlighting, I am able to keep up payments not only on my daughter's teeth but on my son's after-school coaching in math, neither of which I should like repossessed by the finance company.

As I look back on it, I find the most dispiriting phase of all to have been the long months when those horrible braces made my daughter's mouth look as if it was fastened with zippers. Every time she opened her mouth I was surprised she didn't first pull a slide fastener from left to right. And I expected her some day to mumble, with an agonized look on her face, "My zipper's stuck!"

In all seriousness, the teeth-straightening has been a good investment, and I recommend it to any parent with a snaggle-toothed child, especially a girl. Getting those teeth back inside her mouth made such an improvement in my daughter's looks that now I think there is a chance she will get married, after all.

If it does indeed turn out that we got too cheap a job, and the poor girl's teeth return to their original contour, I hope by then she will have grabbed a man, and one capable of keeping her teeth in the condition to which she has become accustomed. The next nine hundred dollars will be on him.

X: Smoking

Smoking, as I keep telling my son and daughter, is a stupid habit. It is dirty, unhealthful, inconsiderate, expensive, and dangerous. Every morning, as soon as I have read the headlines about plane crashes, earthquakes, strikes, and revolutions, I search through the paper for new proof that smoking is linked to lung cancer, and for gruesome items about people falling asleep while smoking in bed. These I read aloud at breakfast in my somberest tones.

"Go on and smoke," I say to my children, after reading the final paragraph, about the sorrowing survivors. "At least you'll escape lung cancer if you burn yourself up first." I can be mighty sarcastic.

"The Yankees won another game," my son announces, turning the pages of the sports section. At least his fingers haven't turned yellow with nicotine yet, though he may keep them bleached out with some new preparation, such as Nicotoff.

"Pass the toast," my daughter says, failing as usual to add "please." My warnings about the bad effects of smoking don't apply to her, she thinks I think. Actually,

> I know she smokes. I've seen my pet
> Light up and draw and blow.
> But innocence remains. As yet
> She doesn't know I know.

Probably I should be proud that my teen-agers are not easily frightened by my horror stories. I'm the coward in the family, carrying a small atomizer with which I nervously spray my throat after inhaling air contaminated by smokers.

"After all, it's *my* life," my son says, and I am forced to agree with him. I just hate to be in the position of an accomplice when I furnish him the money to buy the seeds, or leaves, of his destruction. The time I cut him off for a while, it did no good, because he simply borrowed from his friends, and his friends mostly smoked a brand of cigarettes which, according to the surveys, contained 30 per cent more nicotine and tars than the brand he had been buying for himself.

What added to my embarrassment about my son's borrowing was that my daughter, who keeps our hall closet full of other people's notebooks and megaphones and car coats, was already known throughout high school as "Mooch."

But back to my efforts to frighten my offspring out of the cigarette habit. I do not give up easily. Having failed with terror tactics, I try ridicule.

"Imagine," I say, "what creatures from another planet would think if they were to visit the earth and see people burning little fires under their noses and sucking in the smoke and then blowing it in other people's faces." Then, leaving space fiction and taking a sociological tack, I go on to expound my theory that it is not the smoke of factories or the exhaust from automobiles that causes smog in the modern metropolis. Smog is cigarette smoke, I am convinced. What is needed is a filter that will prevent the smoker from exhaling. This, I am certain, would cut down air pollution, though it might take some of the pleasure out of smoking.

I have developed all this into a pretty good story, with a nice bit of pantomime, and it invariably gets a laugh out of my children.

"Come on, Dad. Give us that smoking routine," they beg, when a bunch of their friends are over at the house. Tired of listening to records, and finding nothing but educational programs on TV, they are desperate for entertainment. Lighting up, they clus-

ter around me expectantly, as if in a night club. My
son tells me that I am their favorite local sick come-
dian, the poor man's Mort Sahl.

"Not right now," I say. "I'm not in the mood for
it." The truth is that I'm like a politician being
drafted for President. I like to be begged a little. It
gives me the feeling of being wanted, if not indis-
pensable.

Usually I oblige, after the proper amount of coaxing, since the evangelist in me hopes that at least
one poor soul may get the message and go straight.
Occasionally a confirmed smoker has seemed to

hesitate, or look a little uneasy, before lighting up and taking a deep drag, then exhaling slowly through the nostrils, with a satisfied look on his face that, frankly, makes me a little envious.

The reason I am so bitter, I guess, is that smoking is just about the only bad habit I have been able to avoid, and therefore the only one I can self-righteously preach against. Drinking, in an unspectacular way, I have succumbed to. And leering at women. And cracking my knuckles. But not smoking. When you have only one small virtue, you have to make the most of it:

I do not smoke. That may be why
I mutter slightly when I buy
The cigarettes for those who do
And empty out their ash trays, too.

When I was a boy, I tried all the wicked things because they were wicked, and that included smoking. Along with my daring contemporaries, I made cigarettes out of corn silk, rolled up in strips of newspaper. Later I dissected cigarette butts and shook out the tobacco for a homemade smoke. After that, I got hold of Cubebs and other ready-made but innocuous cigarettes, the smoking equivalent of 3.2 beer. But I never worked up to honest-to-goodness adult brands. After a few devilish orgies in the neighborhood hideaway, I had finished my experimentation with this particular sin and moved on to others, which held my interest longer.

Teen-agers today skip right over the corn-silk-and-newspaper stage and the dissected-cigarette-butts stage. It is taken for granted that they *have* to smoke; the only question is which brand. In fact, according to the TV commercials if teen-agers don't smoke they don't think for themselves, aren't living modern, and don't go where the action is. Moreover, those chain-smoking athletes in the ads make it pretty plain that unless you smoke you will have no muscles, no endurance, and no girl friends.

"Smoke good, like a teen-ager should," I said one

day to my daughter, when she came in, reeking of cigarette smoke, while I was watching a TV cigarette commercial with my customary fascination.

"That's not very funny," she said, walking up to the TV set and switching to the program of her choice. Sometimes I think she is no more perceptive about humor than she is about grammar, having been schooled in the one by television comics and in the other by television announcers.

Probably the greatest thing about smoking, to a teen-ager, is that it is a sign of maturity. As such, it is almost as effective as a beard, which is a sign of maturity that is very difficult for some teen-agers to achieve, especially girls.

Then too, smoking gives teen-agers something to do with their hands. Otherwise they might nervously unravel a sweater or break the neck off a Coke bottle or strangle a friend.

Once I read an article that explained the desire to smoke as a reversion to infancy, sucking on a cigarette being an unconscious imitation of nursing. I told my daughter about this, thinking it would shame her out of the habit. But all I got from her was, "Don't be disgusting!" Whereupon she lit up another cigarette and blew the smoke in my face. She always has the last word in an argument, especially when I find it difficult to breathe.

In the old days, the approved method of killing off a youngster's desire to smoke was to give him a

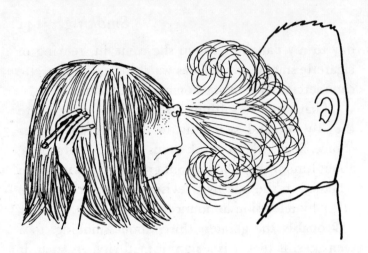

big fat cigar when he showed the first signs of interest in the evil weed, and encourage him, or even
force him, to smoke it down to the last soggy inch.
The youthful smoker was supposed to turn green,
become violently ill, and thereafter have a violent
antipathy toward tobacco.

Like so many fathers before me, I gave it a try.

"Have a stogie?" I said casually to my son, one day
when I thought I detected the odor of tobacco smoke
on him. He was then nine years old, and I wanted to
be sure to catch him before the habit had him in a
firm grip.

"Sure," he said. "Got a match?" He bit off the
end, as he had seen strong, silent men do in the
movies, and expectantly held the long black five-cent
cigar clenched in his teeth until I struck a match and
lifted the flame into position. My hand trembled
just a little. It was a dirty trick to play on a little boy.

Meanwhile I was nervously calculating his distance from the bathroom.

But, as you probably have guessed if you have had any experience with the present generation—a tougher breed than its predecessors—he smoked the cigar down until I had to grab the butt away from him, fearful lest he burn his fingers.

"Got another?" he asked.

I did not try the cigar routine on my daughter. Perhaps I should have. It might have had the desired effect. On the other hand, it might have whetted her appetite at an early age, and today she would be smoking White Owl panatelas instead of mentholated filter tips.

There are, however, a few other carefully tested methods of discouraging a teen-ager from smoking, and I pass these along to parents who think enough of their children to make a serious effort. Those who think their children aren't worth it might at least consider the financial savings involved—as much as twenty-five or fifty cents (for two-pack smokers) a day.

One way is to set a good example and not smoke— even if you have hitherto been a chain smoker and it almost kills you to stop. Regardless of whether this has the desired effect on your teen-ager, it will make you feel like a martyr, which is worth a great deal if you happen to like the feeling.

Another way is to set a bad example by smoking

furiously and incessantly, even if you have never smoked before and hate every minute of it. At every opportunity, shove your face close to his (or hers) and empty your smoke-filled lungs, meanwhile coughing like a consumptive. When your eyes glaze over and your tongue becomes thick and your hands tremble so that you can't pick up a glass of water, the repulsiveness of the habit may dawn on your teen-ager.

"I'll do *anything*, if only you'll quit!" he will cry, dropping to his knees in a touching gesture of filial love and devotion. On the other hand, he may simply leave home and go to live with a relative who smokes with moderation. Whatever he does, you yourself may become an inveterate smoker and find you have been missing something and wish you had started sooner.

Still another way is to promise your child a thousand dollars if he will not smoke until he is twenty-one. You may have to do a little bargaining, perhaps winding up with an offer of ten thousand if he holds off until he is eighteen (he is now seventeen). Once the bargain is sealed, unless you are more trusting than most parents you will have to check on him night and day, snooping and sniffing. This will take a good deal of your time, but when it is all over you may be able to earn back the ten thousand, over a period of years, by working nights as a private detective.

There are other ways, but these are as good as any. As for which is best, I can truthfully say, after having tried each of them, that they will all have just about the same effect. They will do no good whatsoever.

XI: Drinking

I remember the first time I had a beer with my father. I was twenty-seven years old.

"Well, son," my father said, lifting his glass, "here's how."

"Here's how," I repeated, trying to sound like a man. My hand trembled a little, shaking up the beer and sending a trickle of suds down over my wrist.

Not until I had taken my first sip was I able to look up from my glass and face my father, man (at last) to man. When I did, I noticed that his hand had been shaking too, and he was wiping the foam off his shirt cuff. It had been a tense moment for both of us.

"Have another?" my father asked. He tried to sound nonchalant. Now he knew I drank, but he did not know how much.

"No thanks," I said, though it was a hot day and it was draft beer and I could have used another. "One's plenty."

My father was obviously relieved. His son was a man, but not a drunk. It was a great day in the family.

It didn't happen like this with my son and me. In the first place, he wasn't twenty-seven. He was maybe seventeen. I was sitting in the kitchen, drinking beer from a can, when my son came in, opened the refrigerator, took out a can of beer, punched two holes in the top, and sat down at the table opposite me. Lifting the can and tilting back his head, he took a long drink.

"Ahh-h," he sighed with satisfaction, wiping the corners of his mouth with the back of his hand. "Really hits the spot."

Not knowing quite what to say, I just sat there, uncomfortably, while he polished off his beer in a couple of long, gurgling swigs and then got up.

"Gotta be going," he said as he walked out the back door, leaving his beer can on the table for me to dispose of.

I had looked forward to the day my son and I would have our first beer together, but I had thought it would be a little more of a ceremony, or occasion,

than this. Anyhow, now I knew my son drank, and I also knew why the several six-packs of beer I stored in the refrigerator lasted such a short time. I had been blaming the cleaning woman.

In general, there are two ways with which parents may approach the problem of teen-age drinking. In our family my wife believes in one of these ways and I believe in the other, which is not unusual.

My wife would keep all alcoholic beverages out of the house, thus removing temptation from the younger members of the family. This is easier for some parents than for others, especially for teetotalers. My wife is what might be called a semi-teetotaler.

"I don't object to drinking," she says, "it's the *people* who drink. They depress me. Especially the ones who drink too much."

Too much, to her, is more than one glass. When we entertain, she keeps the drinking down by bustling up to a guest who is expectantly holding out an empty glass, taking it from him, and before he can say, "I'm drinking Scotch and soda" or "Yes, I'd like another," engaging him in a lively conversation that lasts until dinner is on the table. Or, if he won't talk, she takes his order, saunters off with his glass, and fails to come back. A variation on this is to return to the thirsty guest, but with bourbon instead of Scotch, or with a tray of hors d'oeuvres. Strongly as she feels about too much drinking, she has no objection to overeating.

One way to keep liquor handy, but out of sight, is to stash it in a secret place in the basement or garage. Another is to store it, with seals and identifying tags, at the home of a neighbor who either has no teen-agers or doesn't care. Since we have no such neighbors, our preacher living on one side of us and a member of Alcoholics Anonymous on the other, we have to keep our liquor in our own house. After having failed dismally in our efforts to keep the hiding place a secret (though the cache in the false bottom of the dishwasher was undiscovered for several months), we were forced to use a locked cabinet with heavy, pry-proof doors. This brought up the problem of where to hide the key.

"Under the rug," my wife suggested.

"Too easy," I said. "How about inside the flush tank of the bathroom toilet?"

"No," my wife said, "I'm not going to reach down in that cold water every time I want the key."

"Inside the fireplace, then, between a couple of bricks in the back of the chimney, up just out of sight," I proposed, having read a good deal of Poe and Dumas and Robert Louis Stevenson in my youth.

That was the first place we hid the key, but after a few times of scraping my clean shirt cuffs against the sooty bricks, I agreed with my wife that some other place might be more practical. So we shifted to another spot, and then another, and I became a bit confused. I recall the time, about a year ago, only an hour before some of our hardest-drinking friends were arriving for cocktails and dinner, when I forgot where I had hidden the key (in my stud box, actually), and had to make a fast trip to the liquor store for emergency supplies. That is why we shifted to a wall safe, though now I am fearful of talking in my sleep and giving away the combination.

"If they don't see it, they won't think of it," my wife says. This is the heart of the no-temptation theory, which for a while caused us to prohibit comic books and to refuse to buy a TV set. The theory would probably work if applied unanimously throughout the world—like universal disarmament. But when we discovered that our children read comic books and watched TV elsewhere, we finally broke down and admitted these instruments of the Devil into our home. Now we all watch TV together, as long as my wife and I are willing to watch *Captain Kangaroo* and *Lassie*. In time I may learn to read a comic book and watch TV simultaneously, as my children do. After all, I was the oldest person in our town to master a hula hoop.

Along with the no-temptation method goes, inevitably, the no-example bit, since the idea is not only to keep teen-agers from knowing about liquor but, above all, to keep them from seeing their parents enjoying it. This will explain to my friends why I sometimes furtively left a party, even at our own house, and took my drink into a clothes closet, shutting the door after me. Drinking in such cramped quarters, with wire coat hangers jabbing at my neck and with the reek of mothballs in my nostrils, somehow dulled my enthusiasm for even the best-mixed martini.

The opposite of no-example is, of course, good-example. On the good-example kick, I have eaten vegetables until I was green in the face, gone to bed early when I was just beginning to enjoy myself, taken a bath when I really didn't need one, gone through a rigorous routine of calisthenics when it was none too good for my heart, and put money into a savings account when I should have bought something that would not have been whittled away by inflation, such as diamond cuff links or a trip to Tahiti. But most painful of all, I have had to pass up a shot of whiskey when I felt pneumonia coming on, meanwhile giving a lecture on the value of vitamin C in the prevention of colds.

So much for the methods favored by my wife, which were the first ones we tried and the first we gave up.

The approach to teen-age drinking which I advocated was to have liquor openly around the house all the time and get the children accustomed to it as something normal and natural, thus denying them the pleasure of being sneaky about it.

"Liquor of all kinds," I told my wife, "should be right out where they can see it. We should have cocktails every day, and wine with dinner. And we should teach our children how to mix and serve drinks."

"All you care about," my wife said, picking up this last point, "is saving the cost of a bartender when we throw a big party."

"That's not so," I protested. "Knowing how to mix drinks is part of a young person's education."

"My mother and father never taught *me*, and I was not irreparably damaged," she said.

"I beg to differ," I said. "It may not have hurt

you, but it embarrassed me plenty when you said to
Ralph Johnson, in front of everybody, that you
thought the best part of a martini was the cherry. It's
a Manhattan that has a cherry in it. A martini has
an olive or an onion. Will you *ever* get them
straight?"

I shouldn't have brought this up, and I apologized
a couple of days later, as soon as she started speaking
to me again.

As a first step in trying my own plan, I brought our
liquor stock out of hiding and put it in plain sight.
Not only did I place bottles of Scotch and bourbon,
along with mixers, jiggers, swizzle sticks, and glasses,
on the dining room buffet, but I interspersed bottles
of gin and vodka among the volumes on the bookshelves in the living room, and set up a row of li-
queurs—crème de menthe, apricot brandy, black-
berry cordial, curaçao, and sundry exotic imports—
on top of the piano. As I added to the array, warm-
ing to my task, the house began to look like a bar,
and I heightened the illusion by keeping the lights
turned so low you had to grope your way around.

My son rather liked the way things looked.

"It's real neat," he said. "I want the guys to see
this."

I was considering adding a juke box and maybe a
slot machine, when my daughter, to my surprise,
said she was embarrassed.

"My friends are nice girls. They come from good

homes," she said. "I'll not have them thinking my parents are a couple of lushes."

Despite this unexpected development, I moved on to the next phase. I persuaded my wife that we should let our daughter learn her capacity. Otherwise she might drink too much, some night when she was out on a date, and her escort might take advantage of her.

"Lips that touch liquor," I said, growing poetic, "touch others' quicker. And once they get started—"

"Oh, no!" my wife exclaimed. "She would never do anything like that." But her imagination is lively, and scenes of drunken debauchery rose to haunt her. By the time she had thought it over for a while, she was convinced that it might already have happened, and worried only lest we were too late with our teaching.

So it was that I tested my daughter's capacity, starting with beer and progressing through sherry and up to whiskey and gin.

That, I should say, was my intention. We got through the beer all right, stopping after three cans when she agreed she had had enough. The sherry test seemed an easy one, but I regret to say that I still do not know my daughter's limit, and trust she does not either, with this mild drink.

You see, somewhere along the line I conked out. I vaguely remember being dragged to bed by my wife, feeling pretty awful.

My daughter tells me she finished up the last of the glass of sherry I had barely begun. She is a thrifty girl, taking after her mother, and hates to waste anything inexpensive. Though I don't know my daughter's capacity for sherry, she knows mine. Consequently, I have given up sherry drinking entirely. I never liked the stuff anyhow.

So there you have two approaches to the problem of teen-age drinking, my wife's and mine, and I commend them both to you. You will be amazed at what you will learn about your offspring and about yourself if you try either of them.

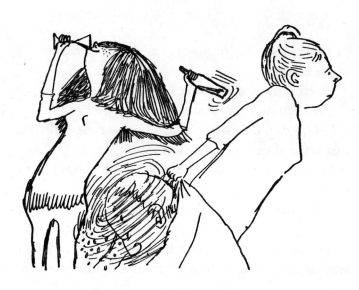

XII: Sex

"I think it's time for you to tell him," my wife said to me one day.

"Tell him what?" I asked.

"You know," she said.

"No, I don't," I said, though by this time I did and just wanted to hear what she would say.

"About s-e-x," my wife said. She's a very good speller.

"All right," I said. "I will."

I didn't say when, however, and several years passed before I got around to it, and my son by then was sixteen. It took that long for me to discuss the

matter with psychologist, biologist, and physician friends, send off for the books and pamphlets they recommended, and prepare my speech. It was also necessary to find the right moment, when my son and I were alone and in a friendly mood.

The hour at last was at hand. I hoped I could remember all the points I planned to make without referring to my notes.

"Son," I began, "I want to talk to you about something."

"O.K.," he said. "Let's have it. What have I done now?"

"It's not about anything you've done," I said, and I hoped this was true. "It's about sex."

"Oh, that," he said, obviously relieved. "What about it?"

Somehow I couldn't recall the rather clever opening remark I had planned, calculated to set my son at ease. Anyhow, he seemed at ease already. What I needed was something to set *me* at ease. I decided to take another tack.

"Have you any questions?" I asked. This was what I had intended for the conclusion of my prepared talk. It was IX. B. 4. of my outline.

"Like what?" he asked.

"Just anything," I said. I thought of asking a probing question myself, such as "Are you for or against it?" but I didn't. "Well," I asked again, "any questions?"

"No," he said.

There was a long silence. Having given the end of my speech, I found it hard to go back to the beginning and take up Point One. Also it seemed awkward to reach into my coat pocket for my notes, the more so because they were in the pocket of a coat that was upstairs in my closet.

"Anything else?" my son asked. "I've got a date tonight."

"With whom?" I asked.

"Leonora," he said.

"Leonora," I repeated thoughtfully, letting the name glide sensuously over my tongue. I could see her in my mind's eye, where, as a matter of fact, she kept turning up frequently, ever since I saw her at the school dance in that tight-fitting dress with the interesting neckline. I remember asking one of the boys who she was. I was a chaperone, and it was not only my right but my duty to know.

"Leonora," the boy said, and rolled his eyes and rubbed his palms. "You sure can pick 'em, Pops."

Extricating myself, reluctantly, from my thoughts, I returned to the matter at hand. "I guess that's all," I said. I had a feeling that my son knew the basic facts of life. Anything more advanced, he could find out better from Leonora than from me. After all, didn't this Modern Education emphasize on-the-job training, learning by doing, and all that sort of thing?

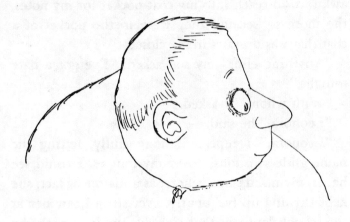

So I resolved, forthwith, to worry no more about my son—neither where he went nor whom he went with. It took a great load off my mind:

> No longer do I sit up till
>   My teen-age son comes in,
> And stay awake with rod-like will
>   Though drooping eyes and chin.
>
> At last, as I have proudly said,
>   I've gained some trust and sense.
> I nonchalantly go to bed—
>   And lie there taut and tense.

When I was young, my father never talked to me about sex, though I am sure he must have known about it. As for my mother, she avoided the subject after one unsuccessful attempt to inform me in the way she had been informed by *her* mother.

"What do you know about the birds and the bees?" she asked me, when I was about ten.

"Quite a bit," I said proudly, because I happened at that time to belong to the Audubon Society and to have a friend whose father kept honey bees.

So I gave her quite a lecture about the snowy egret and the yellow-throated warbler and the belted kingfisher and the crested screamer, and I explained how bees obtain nectar from flowers and turn it into honey and how beekeepers keep from getting stung by blowing smoke into hives with bee smokers and wearing bee veils over their heads.

I didn't get around to where the birds come from and where the bees come from, because I wasn't any too clear about this, and my mother never brought up the subject again. Even if I had known, I would have seen no similarity between, say, larvae and babies. How ridiculous can you get?

My knowledge about sex came finally, and tardily, from a little book, written in simple, restrained language and containing a few sketchy drawings. The title, as I recall, was *How Babies Are Born*. It was a real shocker, and I was so afraid it would be discovered by my parents, and confiscated and burned, that I didn't dare bring it into the house. I wrapped it in an old newspaper and hid it under some bushes in the city park, and when I went there to read it I felt thoroughly wicked. After a heavy rain it got all soggy and came to pieces in my hands. Unable to secure another copy, I was left to go it alone, doubtful that I could remember all those incredible things without looking them up occasionally.

But times have changed, even if sex hasn't. Now the only way a boy of ten can escape a thorough sex education is by never going to a movie or watching TV or reading about love nests and rape cases on the front page of the home-delivered local paper. A book such as I hid in the bushes could not possibly compete with the paperbacks available at any supermarket or drugstore.

When I was in high school, and even in college, the only term I ever heard for fooling around with girls was "necking." The word probably derived from the fact that such activity was limited to the anatomical area from the Adam's apple up.[1] But now there is a carefully defined series of terms, starting with "necking" and "making out" and progressing to "petting" and "going all the way." Once a girl steps into a car with a boy, especially when they are beginning to get serious about each other—say on their second date—the only question is when the wrestling will begin:

> A girl in a car
> With a boy knows this much:
> His foot's on the brake,
> But his mind's on the clutch.

Oh yes, they had cars when I was a boy, but they didn't have drive-in movies. And did you ever try asking a boy and a girl what the movies were about, when they have come back from a drive-in after a double feature that lasted four hours?

"One of them was a Western, I think," the boy may say.

[1] In view of all the goings-on in the Garden of Eden, "Adam's appling" might be a better word than "necking."

"And Debbie Reynolds was in the other one," the girl may manage, since she got a few glimpses out of the corner of her eye.

One thing girls were good at in my day, and are still plenty skillful about when they want to be, is the technique of distracting boys, at the right time or sooner, with diversionary tactics.

I don't know how it's done, because I am not and never have been a girl, but I know it *is* done. The nearest parallel I can think of is a bullfighter and how he draws off a rampaging bull with a flick of his cape. The similarity between a bull and a charging, predatory teen-age boy is pretty close, too.

My wife or some knowledgeable friend has, I am sure, given our daughter some coaching about the

timely coughing fit, the accidental leaning on the car horn, and the frightened whisper, effected with histrionics worthy of Eleanora Duse or Sarah Bernhardt. "Did you hear someone calling?" she asks, or "Don't look now, but—" For my part, I have given our son a few helpful hints also:

> My father's father told my father
> The proper things to do.
> My father told them then to me;
> I tell them now to you.

> My father's father, father, I,
> Now you, know right from wrong.
> We may not always do it, but
> We pass the word along.

If there is one thing that worries parents more than anything else, a kind of superworry, it is the crazy business of going steady, especially when the youngster is only a sophomore or junior in high school, and the Big Love is a featherbrained girl or an unpromising lout of a boy. When two sixteen-year-olds start acting like man and wife, it's pretty frightening.

And parents are helpless. The more they talk against it, and threaten disinheriting, disinfecting, or whatever, the more they drive the two soulmates together. Moving to another country is rather difficult, since it means cleaning out the garage, selling your home and business, learning a strange language, and starting a new career in middle age. It might be worth it, however, except for the likelihood that your child will find another Big Love, and a more impossible one, maybe with a mustache, in another country.

Going steady is, of course, only the beginning of the end:

> When boys and girls start going steady,
>> Their parents' look is drawn.
> They know that it's a case of going,
>> Going, going, gone.

One of my friends, poor fellow, has three daughters, aged sixteen, seventeen, and eighteen. Usually two of them, and sometimes all three, are going steady, and with boys who turn his stomach when he so much as hears their names. But he and his wife have managed to break off each new romance after a few months, while it was still breakable, and without antagonizing their daughters.

"How do you do it?" I asked him admiringly.

"Simple," he said. "By overexposure."

"What do you mean?" I asked, hoping his method was not as bad as it sounded.

"Well, we have a beach house," he said. "When one of the girls gets to going steady with some obnoxious pipsqueak, we invite him to spend a long week end with us—and I'm telling you it's long. It seems like years."

"Then what?"

"We keep the boy and our daughter together every possible hour, morning till night. Not all night— we have to draw the line somewhere—but all the rest of the time. We get them up early and hustle them to breakfast together, and give him the sports section to read while they eat. We send them on long walks down the beach. And we keep them up late, insisting that they play game after game of parcheesi. We do our best to help him win every time, and maybe give just the slightest impression of cheating. As I say, it's a long week end, but it works."

"How does it work?" I asked.

"She gets tired of him. Or he gets tired of her. Or they get tired of each other at about the same time. My wife and I get tired of the whole thing after the first couple of hours, but we are desperate people and we stick with it. The main thing is that when we go back to town she's through going steady, at least with that one. It may be a lost week end, but it's also a lost boy friend."

I am glad I had this little talk with my friend, because otherwise we might never have bought a house at the beach. I had wanted a beach house for years, but my wife stubbornly said we couldn't afford it, and she was right. However, when I told her of the dramatic successes achieved by my friend's overexposure technique, she gave in. Anything to get rid

of the current callow youth to whom our daughter clings but whom we wouldn't touch with gloves on:

> She holds his hand, she looks adoring.
> His platitudes are never boring.
> No doubt some boys are greener, sappier—
> Tell me of one, and I'll be happier.

So we bought the beach house. And the very first week end we went there, we took our daughter's boy friend along. We could hardly wait to get started on The Cure.

"Do you think we can stay with it from Friday afternoon to Sunday evening?" I asked my wife, doubtfully.

"Chin up," she said. "People have gone without food and water longer than that."

She is a resolute woman, of pioneer stock. And she will do almost anything to insure a successful marriage for her daughter, a successful marriage being one which brings us a son-in-law with brains, looks, and—I always put in when she overlooks it—money or the prospect of earning it.

I remember the week end well. It was the latter part of June, and our daughter's boy friend had just graduated from high school, without, however, learning anything about English grammar or good manners. He was a boy with an unusual face—the kind you are not likely to forget, no matter how hard you try—his head coming to such a sharp point that it would have punched a hole in a cap, and his chin curling forward and upward in such a way that it imperiled his nose when he shut his mouth, which he did all too seldom. The most remarkable thing about him was probably his forehead—he didn't have any, just a series of creases between his eyebrows and his hairline.

My daughter thought he looked so much like Gregory Peck it was astonishing, and I thought it was astonishing she thought so. I spent forty-five dollars on an oculist before I discovered this was nothing glasses would help and I should have been spending my money on a psychiatrist.

That first Friday afternoon at the beach I tried to get acquainted with the boy, hoping to learn what it was my daughter saw in him, since it couldn't possibly be his looks.

"What college are you going to?" I asked, just to make conversation.

"I'm not going to college," he said. "It don't help to study any more when you've been to a real fine school like Central High. What would I learn?"

"Nothing, I guess," I said, and I meant it.

We got through the week end all right. Well, not all right but reasonably intact, except for a nervous tic I developed in my right eyelid.

The main thing is that the romance was shattered. It would never be the same again. I mean the romance between my wife and me. You see, she actually began to like the boy, or at least to defend him, and to be annoyed with me for failing to see his good qualities.

"He's really very sweet," she said.

"So is honey," I said, "but that's no reason for my daughter to marry a drone."

"He'll earn a good living," she said.

"Doing what?" I asked. "Sweeping streets, maybe, if he ever figures out which end of a broom is the handle."

"There you go again," she said, "always the snob.

As a matter of fact he already has a job for the rest of the summer."

"I must admit I'm surprised and encouraged," I said. "Where is he working and how soon does he start?"

"He's working for us, starting Monday," she said. "I've told him he could stay in the beach house all summer and look after it, and we'll pay for his food and give him a little spending money."

I was so mad I couldn't even ride back from the beach in the same car with my wife. I rode the bus, a four-hour trip with two changes.

Now we have a beach house on our hands that it will take twenty years to pay for and that I swear I'll never go into again.

And my daughter's steady, who looks more and more like my future son-in-law, has at last found himself professionally. He has become a first-rate beachcomber. I never thought he would work as hard as he does, picking up candy wrappers and beer cans, most of which he has tossed onto the beach himself. Now and then, I am told, he finds an unusual shell or a curiously shaped piece of driftwood, which he brings into the house and places on display in the bookshelves. Where the books have gone, no one seems to know.

From reports I get, the boy takes quite an interest, a proprietary interest, in the place. He gives people the impression he owns it; and the way things are going, in a few years he will. Though I have not seen the house for several months, I understand from the grocery bills that there is a gay, hospitable air about it. Apparently it is always full of people—his friends. My wife and daughter continue to go down on week ends. When there is no room for them, they stay at a nearby motel, which is quite comfortable.

The odd thing about it is that this brassy youth, this pin-headed, illiterate Gregory Peck, thinks I like him. "Dear Pop," he writes me, "We all miss you. Hear are this months grocary bills. Love." If I were to tell him what I really think of him, I would lose my wife completely. So I get what satisfaction I can out of writing him vicious letters which, once they are carefully written and placed in a stamped envelope, I tear up. I have learned to put the stamp on lightly, so that I am able to remove it and use it again.

I have to save every penny for the payments on that beach house, for those grocery bills, and for the wedding that I fear is not far off.

Looking ahead, I can imagine my wife smilingly saying to friends and well-wishers at the wedding reception, "No, we haven't lost a daughter, we've gained a son." She is a courageous woman, in public, as well as a user of clichés. But once the newlyweds have driven off (in our car) and the last guest has gone, she will break down and let the tears come.

And when I think of the son I have gained, so will I.

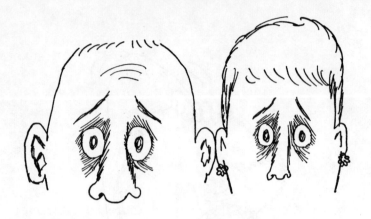

Epilogue

Several years have passed since I began this treatise on teen-agers. The world is about the same as ever, or a little worse, and adolescence, which I have already described as a disease, has broken out everywhere in an especially virulent form. It has, indeed, reached epidemic proportions. Almost everyone between twelve and twenty has it bad. Despite spectacular successes in other areas, medical science continues to be helpless.

To quote one baffled M.D., looking up wearily from his microscope, "We are helpless."

But time heals all wounds. We have taken down the Health Department sign, WARNING: THIS HOUSEHOLD IS AFFLICTED WITH ADOLESCENCE, which for so many years greeted guests and tradesmen as they stepped up to ring our front doorbell. We have opened the windows wide and given the house a good airing, having been assured that fumigation was unnecessary.

You see, our young people, now not quite so young, have both left home. Our son went into the Army, and at last is getting all he can eat. He is also, I am told, keeping his room straightened up. And he comes when he is called. This proves either that he is no longer a teen-ager or that he should have been drafted when he was thirteen.

As for our daughter, she is married and living in a home of her own, or one that will be her own in fifteen years if we continue keeping up our share of the monthly payments. Despite all my fears, she did not marry the goon to whom she was overexposed at the beach house. He disappeared one day, I think carried out by the tide. We notified the police, but if they ever found him, they were nice enough not to tell me.

The most astonishing thing is not that our two teen-agers have ceased being teen-agers, or that they have left home, but that we miss them.

Now I have only my wife to disagree with, and this has become monogamous. Lacking my teen-agers to irritate me, I irritate myself, which is unwholesome and unnatural. I've never been the do-it-yourself type.

The phone seldom rings, and this gives the house an eerie stillness and makes us feel cut off from the world. Also, the phone is always available. For a while I kept phoning everyone I could think of, luxuriating in this freedom of communication. But, except for a few interesting wrong numbers, the novelty soon wore off. And there were subtle indications, such as the click of the receiver after my cheery "Hello, Bob" or "Guess who this is," that my friends were getting less and less of a thrill out of hearing from me.

The bathroom, too, is always unoccupied, and I can go in and shave any old time. This was fine for a while, but I developed a painful skin rash from raking my cheeks six or seven times a day. I began to pull the door shut when I went out and pretend someone was in there. Just for old times' sake, I would even beat on the door and rattle the doorknob and yell, "Aren't you ever coming out?" But it was a hollow performance of which I soon tired, especially when I had just shaved. Other people can fool me easily, but I have a hard time fooling myself.

Also, when I am at a dinner party, I am beginning to lose the self-discipline built up over years of not having ready access to the bathroom. I refer to the discipline that enabled me to smile, in a superior way, and shake my head, when my hostess asked me, as the evening wore on, "Wouldn't you like to freshen up a bit? It's the second door on the left."

But one of the strangest things I have noticed is how the closets suddenly and miraculously have grown larger. There is room to hang all my clothes, and space left over. I mentioned this curious phenomenon to my wife.

"Yes," she said. "In fact the whole house is larger, and kind of empty. We'll have to buy some more furniture."

"No, not that," I put in hastily. "It would be cheaper to close off a few rooms. Save on heat, too."

As for cars, our daughter took hers with her, but that leaves us two. Now there is no need for me to go shopping on my bicycle, pedaling back up the hill with the wire basket full of groceries. In an amazingly short time I have gained fifteen pounds, all in the same area.

Of course, I had a little trouble with the car at first. It had been so long since I was at the wheel that I had to get used to some of the newer developments, such as the push-button radio.

"Look at this," I said to my wife, when I pulled on a knob on the dashboard, out of curiosity. "A cigarette lighter! What will they think of next?"

Somehow, the fun has gone out of mowing the lawn, without my muscular son watching me and urging me on. And now that I can listen to my favorite news commentator on television at 6:00 P.M., I rather miss the program running from 5:00 to 7:00 that held my daughter enthralled—the movies star-

ring Norma Shearer and Leslie Howard and Lionel Barrymore that I always came in at the middle of and could only vaguely recall having seen thirty years ago.

And now that my children's friends no longer drop in at unexpected hours, I have no reason for keeping more or less properly dressed so that my son and daughter will not feel ashamed of me when I answer the doorbell in the ragged sweater and paint-spattered pants I like to lounge around in. The challenge of icy appraisal by a carload of girls, come to pick my daughter up to go to a party, is gone, and I fear I shall soon look threadbare and be unable, from lack of trying, to pull my stomach in.

In short, I feel like a prizefighter, toughened by ten years of wins, losses, and draws, who has suddenly run out of opponents. At last he has bought the little farm he has dreamed about and saved for, but he isn't as happy as he had anticipated.

My wife and I do a good deal of reminiscing, sometimes becoming pretty sentimental.

"Here is Jeff," my wife said one day as we were looking through a photograph album, "with his first traffic citation."

"And here is Karin," I said, "with what's-his-name, the sailor in Hawaii. You know, the one we had to tell not to come around any more."

"Oh, *that* one," my wife said, and a shudder ran through her.

"And here are Jeff and Karin together," I said. "I never could get a good picture of the two of them at once. Usually one looks good and the other doesn't. This time they both look terrible."

"My, what memories these pictures bring back," my wife said, her eyes misting slightly. "Don't you wish the children were young again, just beginning their teens, and we could go through those years all over?"

Her question touched me deeply. I patted her tenderly and consolingly on the shoulder. Then I thought back over the years, and a host of incidents crowded my mind. A lump formed in my throat.

Finally I answered her question.

"No," I said.

Twisted Tales from Shakespeare   Armour

This book has been bought by about 100,000 non-, anti-, and even pro-Shakespearean scholars. It is now reprinted because both the publisher and the author have heard that (1) world population is well over 3,000,000,000 (including astronauts), and (2) there is a population explosion.

The Table of Contents lists Shakespeare's life and theater, six plays — Hamlet, Macbeth, A Midsummer Night's Dream, Romeo and Juliet, The Merchant of Venice, Othello — and the Sonnets. Nevertheless, the Bard will survive, as have all known readers, cliches about deaths from laughing to the contrary notwithstanding.

Golf Is a Four-Letter Word
Richard Armour

People who struggle with a problem find
comfort in the knowledge that they are not
alone. If they are caught by the golf habit,
compulsively trudging from tee to green and
green to tee, this is the book they will turn
to. It may not reduce their score, but it will
reduce their guilt complex.

Richard Armour graphically depicts how,
an innocent youth, he was lured into his
addiction to golf; how, still innocent, he gave
himself wholeheartedly to a seemingly
harmless sport; how he became, over the
years, more and more ensnared; how his
wife's suffering and love helped him through
his darkest hours; and finally, as proof of
total cure, how he became so involved in a
new interest that he can now easily resist
his wife's pleas that he return to golf.

The Classics Reclassified Richard Armour

"The Iliad...is about Ilium, which is another name for Troy and not the new chemical added to a toothpaste."

Julius Caesar: "The opening scene is in Rome. A Street. A Street is presumably just north of B Street."

Ivanhoe: "These are the days of chivalry, when people are very courteous about the way they hit each other over the head with staves and run each other through with spears."

The Scarlet Letter: "The letter, which the prisoner fashioned herself with a needle friends smuggled to her in a pincushion, is an 'A'. Apparently she had intended to go through the alphabet...but ran out of thread."

Moby Dick: "'Call me Ishmael,' Melville says. (He had never liked the name Herman.)"

Silas Marner: "What gives weight to George Eliot's moralizing is her having lived in sin all those years with a married man."

David Copperfield: "The story is told in the first person, by David Copperfield, though he is not born until the end of the first chapter."

Catalog

If you are interested in a list of fine Paperback
books, covering a wide range of subjects
and interests, send your name and address,
requesting your free catalog, to:

McGraw-Hill Paperbacks
330 West 42nd Street
New York, New York 10036